Copyright ©2012 by Sonic Reiki Press

All rights reserved. No part of this book may be reproduced, utilized in any form or by any means without prior permission in writing from the publisher.

Second Edition

www.sonicreiki.com

e-mail: soundmaster55@verizon.net

ISBN-13:978-0615668932 (Linda Sylvester)
ISBN-10:0615668933

Printed in the United States of America

Healing the Physical Inner Children

USING QUANTUM CONFIGURATION CHAMBERS
Easily & Effortlessly

LINDA SYLVESTER
Founder of Sonic Reiki

About the Author

Linda teaching in Richmond Hill, Ontario.

Although Linda was born in 1951, she feels her life really began when she had a near death experience in 1980. After having an allergic reaction to a medical injection just before surgery, Linda's heart stopped for six minutes on the operating table. During these six minutes, new life was born. She saw herself going into a bright light. This light was brighter than the brightest star that she ever had seen, and yet this light was only 50 feet away and her eyes never flinched.

Inside Linda's lifeless body, her soul screamed out for help. After being declared dead, a nurse sitting next to the gurney telepathically heard Linda's soul scream. The nurse took a mirror and placed it under Linda's mouth. She yelled to the doctors, "She is still alive!" The doctors then called a "code blue" and used the electric paddles twice while waiting for the resuscitator to be brought down from the third floor. Linda remembers coming back into her body and hearing her own words, "Your work is not yet finished."

After a year of recovery, Linda noticed she could hear sounds that other people couldn't. After putting little bits of information here and there together, she realized she could hear like a dog. Scientists define this range of sound as ultra sound. What Linda was hearing was the sound of people's organs, cells, feelings, etc. This is where Sonic Reiki began to take form. During the first ten years after her near death experience, Linda went back to college and completed her business degree from Bryant and Stratton. From there, she excelled in the business world and became a credit manager for a large international company, while quietly pursuing her metaphysical interest. During that time, she became a Reiki Master Teacher.

In 1995, Linda quit the business world and began to follow her heart's desire. This is when her real work began. The first item on her agenda was to write her book, *Message to the Children of the Light*. In 1996, through special invitation, Linda worked on a special assignment at the United Nations where she met with ambassadors from all over the world. Her mission was to activate the Divine Grid of Unity among Nations. By 1997, Linda was honored with an induction into the Seneca Wolf clan for her community healing work. Over the next few years, Linda appeared on television and radio promoting her advanced healing sound techniques. While teaching at Willow Creek Wellness Center, Linda met Tom.

In the spring of 2000, Tom's car broke down and he needed a way to get to work in Hamburg from West Seneca, NY, which was about 15 miles away. He decided to ride a bicycle to his shop for a few days until his car was fixed. Just about half way to his shop, Tom became tired and thirsty and pulled over to the side of the road for a few minutes. There, he happened to look up and saw a sign for Willow Creek Wellness Center. Tom had been working on his spiritual path for some time and he wanted to take his next step. Intuition told him it that his next spiritual step was going to be at Willow Creek. He made an appointment to see the facility and to see a list of classes being offered. One class jumped out at him: "Chakra Reprogramming." Week after week, the class was cancelled because there weren't enough students to fill the class, but Tom pursued. Mostly because of Tom's persistence, the owner of Willow Creek changed the class policy. A class would be taught even if there was only one student registered.

On July 18, 2000, Linda was out in the Allegany foothills, about 4 miles into the woods, when she was instructed to return to town to teach one student who was registered for her "Chakra Reprogramming" class. Reluctantly, but true to her integrity, she showed up on time to teach her one student.

Spirit works in mysterious ways. On that night, as the room filled with registered students, Linda watched the energies of the room change when the last student appeared. The student went to the desk and asked if the teacher was present. The desk clerk pointed to Linda on the couch. The student sat down next to

Linda and said, "I have been looking for a woman here to teach me...are you her?" Linda paused, and said, "Yes." That student was Linda's Twin Flame, who is now known as her husband, Tom.

Together, Linda and Tom have developed several degree programs specializing in Sonic Reiki, autism, animal healing and Twin Flame counseling. Their journey has allowed them to teach in places such as Hawaii, the Grand Cayman Islands, Toronto, New York City, greater Philadelphia, Pittsburgh, and several areas in Florida.

Their Divine Mission is to teach Sonic Reiki to people who are looking to take their next step on their spiritual path. Sonic Reiki isn't a religion - it is a way of life. One learns compassion when he/she is able to see the big picture, gaining an understanding of how the universe works.

Tribute

To my husband Tom, who is also known as my Twin Flame!

Linda and Tom

There is an incredible feeling when one meets someone who mirrors your deepest dreams. Thank you, Tom, for walking with me on this Divine Path! You have been truly one of my greatest teachers.

Acknowledgements

I wish to personally thank the following people for their contributions to my inspiration and knowledge, and for their help in creating this book:

My husband, Tom
Who is also my twin flame, and my illustrator

My Daughters
Sherri Kiefer
Amy Schnell, my graphic designer, editor, and photographer

Lucinda and Karsten Jensen
My dear friends and inspirational teachers

Past, present and future students
from all around the world

Dave Schnell
For technical support

And my beautiful grandchildren
Julianne, Kimberly, David and Adam

Table of Contents

Chapter 1: What is Sonic Reiki? .... Page 1

Chapter 2: How to Use This Book 5

Chapter 3: How to Find Your Own Truth 7

Chapter 4: Protocol and Intention 9

Chapter 5: How to Tone 11

Chapter 6: What is a Quantum Configuration Chamber? 13

Chapter 7: Physical Inner Children Intents:
- Releasing Jealousy 17
- Releasing Grief 18
- Releasing Denial 19
- Releasing Hatred 20
- Releasing Loneliness 21
- Releasing Anxiety 22
- Releasing Sadness 23
- Releasing the Fear of Being Separated from Mother 24
- Releasing the Fear of Being Separated from Father 25
- Releasing the Fear of Being Separated from Parents 26
- Releasing Naivety 27
- Releasing Helplessness 28
- Releasing Anger 29
- Releasing Resentment 30
- Releasing Guilt 31
- Releasing Passiveness 32
- Releasing Aggressiveness 33
- Releasing Procrastination 34
- Releasing Loss 35
- Releasing Abandonment 36

- Releasing Lack of Discernment 37
- Releasing Reluctance 38
- Releasing the Fear of Being Alone 39
- Releasing Poverty Consciousness 40
- Releasing Needing Approval of Others 41
- Releasing Low Self Esteem 42
- Releasing Low Self Worth 43
- Releasing the Need to Always Please Parents 44
- Releasing the Energy of Being a Pessimistic 45
- Releasing Making the Wrong Decision 46
- Releasing Lack of Confidence 47
- Releasing Panic 48
- Releasing Being Lost 49
- Releasing Illusion 50
- Releasing Embarrassment 51
- Releasing Humiliation 52
- Releasing Shame 53
- Releasing Stupidity 54
- Releasing Rage 55
- Releasing the Bully Within 56
- Releasing the Fear of Someone Close to Me Dying 57
- Releasing the Fear of Being Shunned 58
- Releasing the Fear of Failure 59
- Releasing the Fear of Being Judged 60
- Releasing Aguish 61
- Releasing Despair 62
- Releasing Being Unwanted 63
- Releasing Being Overwhelmed 64
- Releasing the Fear of Being Rejected 65
- Releasing the Fear of Being Ignored 66
- Releasing the Fear of Being Left Behind 67
- Releasing the Fear of Being Attacked 68
- Releasing the Fear of Being Taken Advantage Of 69
- Releasing the Fear of Fire 70
- Releasing the Fear of Water 71

- Releasing the Fear of Heights 72
- Releasing Self Sabotage 73
- Releasing Codependency 74
- Releasing My False Self 75
- Releasing Suffering 76
- Releasing Confusion 77
- Releasing Emptiness 78
- Releasing Unhappiness 79
- Releasing Stubbornness 80
- Releasing Illness 81
- Releasing Rigidity 82
- Releasing Being Emotionally Cold 83
- Releasing Lack of Nurturing 84
- Releasing Bondage 85
- Releasing Neglect 86
- Releasing Being Trapped 87
- Releasing Being a Victim 88
- Releasing Being a Martyr 89
- Releasing Being a Liar 90
- Releasing Being in Danger 91
- Releasing Being Mocked 92
- Releasing Pity 93
- Releasing Disapproval 94
- Releasing Forgetfulness 95
- Releasing Manipulation 96
- Releasing Sorrow 97
- Releasing Rape 98
- Releasing the Fear of Going Home 99
- Releasing the Fear of Being Fat 100
- Releasing the Fear of Being Tortured 101
- Releasing the Fear of Speaking in Front of Large Audiences .. 102
- Releasing Nightmares 103
- Releasing the Fear of Being Robbed 104
- Releasing the Fear of Starving to Death 105
- Releasing the Fear of Spiders 106

- Releasing the Fear of Dying... 107
- Releasing the Fear of Losing Money 108
- Releasing the Fear of Being Homeless 109
- Releasing the Fear of Being Unloved 110
- Releasing Maliciousness... 111
- Releasing Being Controlled 112
- Releasing Thievery 113
- Releasing Carelessness 114

Chapter 8: Nurturing Your Physical Inner Child 115
Chapter 9: Exploring the Physical Inner Childrens' Next Step 117
Testimonials 119

Chapter 1: What is Sonic Reiki?

Sonic Reiki is an ancient and yet cutting edge technology which aligns to the electromagnetic energy spectrum. This allows you to open up to the highest possible reality for healing. The electromagnetic spectrum is a vast band of energy frequencies which extends from radio waves to gamma waves, from the very lowest frequencies to the highest possible frequencies.

Sonic Reiki is a natural alternative therapy whereby people of all ages can benefit from its gentle energy flow.

Sonic Reiki can assist those who suffer from minor ailments such as headaches, muscle strains, insect bites, stomach aches, and everyday stressors. It also can benefit those who suffer from more serious illness such as diabetes, cancer, blood disorders, schizophrenia, post traumatic stress disorders, allergies, emotional issues, sleep disorders, heart issues (physical and emotional), chronic fatigue, and autism. Animals and plants love it too!

After a Sonic Reiki treatment, clients have expressed that they were more relaxed, calm, focused, and energized, even though they felt fatigued before the treatment. They are now sleeping better, have more patience, are less angered, have more creativity, their prosperity has increased, and they were more likely to complete projects.

Energy follows intent. It is the intentions that matter. It doesn't matter how much distance there is between the sender and receiver. Sonic Reiki can benefit everyone, particularly someone who is open to an additional point of view. This expands their awareness of themselves.

Sonic Reiki is an alternative healing therapy which integrates well with other alternative therapies. It is used in massage therapy, reflexology, kinesiology, yoga, and chiropractic therapies, among others.

The most asked question in Sonic Reiki is: "Do I need musical training to be able to practice Sonic Reiki?" The answer is *no*. The tone comes from the heart. The Sonic Reiki practitioner states his or her intent, creates healing chambers, gets his/her protocol, and tones from the heart. The practitioner never knows what sounds come out until they are toned. Neither does the recipient. These sounds and sequences have never been heard the same way twice. This is what creates new neural pathways within the recipient's brain, allowing it to reprogram with a new intent.

Sonic Reiki has the ability to turn gene expressions on and off. A team of research scientists, led by biophysicist Pjotr Garjajev, found that DNA stores data similar to the way a computer stores memory.[1] Their studies show that genetic codes use grammar rules and syntax in a way that closely mirrors human language. In Sonic Reiki, one is taught how to access memory codes, like those used thousands of years ago in Lemuria by those who were telepathic. Once the big picture of the disease patterns are revealed to the Sonic Reiki practitioner (through muscle testing and the art of asking questions), the practitioner uses his/her voice to turn gene expressions on and off. In 2010, Tom and Linda worked with a Polish physicist. Using high tech equipment, the physicist amassed the same information that Linda and Tom obtained via muscle testing. Except Linda and Tom reached the conclusion faster.

Sonic Reiki accelerates one's own healing ability. Why? In Sonic Reiki, we explore both physical and etheric reasons for which disease patterns manifest. Humans are made of over 70% water. Dr. Emoto, a Japanese author known for his studies of water's impact on consciousness, has proven that water holds memory.[2] Sonic Reiki tones awaken memory cells, including past and future memory cells. This includes anything we've mastered in the past and future, which comes forth into the present. When our mastery comes forth, things begin to accelerate. This is very much needed as we step through the time accelerations for 2012 and beyond. For those of you who are just beginning your journey, time is speeding up. Each year, time speeds up twenty times faster than the year before. Last year, you were able to perform and complete 20 tasks per hour with an average amount of stress. It is important to release the blocks within the physical inner child. If this is neglected, people will become overwhelmed as they go through the time accelerations. The great benefit is that this will allow you to perform and complete 40 tasks per hour with an average amount of stress. This is how we will be taking the quantum leap into higher consciousness!

Once a person experiences Sonic Reiki, his/her spirit is awakened. It becomes a way of life as it teaches us to see into the multi-dimensionality of who we are. Our whole journey is to go back home to see who we really are, without illusions, masks and deceptions. The time is NOW!

Chapter 2: How to Use This Book

Muscle test to discover your primary intent.

For instance, let's say your muscle testing shows that *worry* is your primary intent. You would make a list of all the things you worry about: those items you worry about now, and those you have worried about throughout your life. For example, when I did this exercise, my muscle testing showed that I was still worrying about kids stealing my toys at age three. Such patterns can be conscious or subconscious. When you start this list, you'll likely be surprised at how many things you have worried about in your life.

The purpose of this exercise is to release big blocks at once, creating large spaces for which new spiritual information can ground. This is how matter is spiritualized.

Spiritualizing matter is the process of integrating heaven and earth. During this process, matter lifts and beautifies as it begins to electrify its vibratory frequency. This allows humanity to awaken within the highest possible reality for perception.

Intents are meant to transform, transmute, and transfigure the physical, emotional and mental bodies for evolutionary spiritual development.

When you feel you've reached critical mass with your list (of worries, for example), carefully take your list outside and burn it in a safe place. As the list burns, the spirit awakens. The quantum configuration chambers allow space for spirit to spiritualize into matter.

Remember, each day your primary intent will change, and it doesn't necessarily follow the same order as the intents in this book. Keep track of the intents you have done in a little diary.

Enjoy your journey!

Chapter 3: How to Find Your Own Truth

Muscle testing allows us to connect to our Divine Truth. Divine Truth sets us free. To evolve, we need to distinguish our own truth. It's one of the greatest gifts that we have been given. Finding our own truth builds trust. Trust builds self worth and self esteem. As self worth and self esteem raises, so does our prosperity and abundance!

For Example:

If you don't question the validity of truth within a book in which you are reading, your mind accepts the book as truth. That is okay if it is all true. But what if the book is only 50% true? The old saying is "garbage in, garbage out." Sometimes we overhear something we don't understand, and so we don't know what to do with the information. If we muscle test the information and it is true, whether we understand it or not, it gets stored in our spiritual library of knowledge until we can hold the frequency of the information.

Through muscle testing we can:

- Tell if someone is being a wolf in sheep's clothing.
- Ask if it is for the highest possible reality for you to make this financial investment.
- Ask if it is for the highest possible reality for you to change jobs at this time, etc.
- Monitor if we are aligned to our Divine Path.

The possibilities are endless!

Establish Your Own Truth

1. **Check Your Polarity** – While standing, you can ask, "Is my name *(state your name)*?" If your name is correct, you should fall forward. If you don't fall forward when the response is a *yes*, and backwards is a *no*, then your polarity is off.

    Correcting Polarity – Tap just below the knee cap at the reflex point where the doctor taps to see if your reflexes are healthy. Tapping there three times and toning the vowel sound "E" three times with the intent of correcting your polarity usually works. Also, drinking a glass of water helps. After tapping, and ask your name again to see if the polarity has corrected itself. If no, contact us at *soundmaster55@verizon.net* as there might be a deeper issue.

2. **Muscle Testing Technique** – There may be times when standing up to muscle test is not possible. Once you begin to trust your muscle testing you can begin to muscle test sitting down, just like when you learned to walk, the first step was to learn to crawl, therefore, if standing to muscle test is not possible, try this technique.

3. **Create a Circuit** – Connect your left middle finger and left thumb. Then connect your right middle finger and thumb, linking them through your left finger/left thumb connection. If this chain breaks, your answer is *no*. If it stays together your answer is *yes*.

    For example: What if you are in a restaurant and you would like to muscle test if the green beans are good for you? In the collective consciousness, we have been taught that green beans are healthy. What if the cook that day was having a bad day? The cook's energy transfers into the green beans that you thought were healthy for you. Your muscle testing could tell you this before you eat them.

Chapter 4: Protocol and Intention

What is Protocol?

Protocol is a set of questions that create a safeguard to prevent miscreation and/or karma. Asking for permission honors the Universe. As we evolve, this protocol gets more in depth as we learn to ask deeper questions. Before asking questions, beginners should first confirm whether or not the intent is complete.

What is Intent?

Think of your intentions as a Divine Recipe, and think of your Divine Creator Source as the cook. It's important to know that the cook reads the recipe literally. If your intent is, for example, "to want enough money to pay your bills monthly" then the cook will read *want* as *lack*. Consequently, the cook creates lack of money to pay your bills monthly.

The cook sees the field of intent as primary, a field which it responds to when you act upon your intent. For example, if your intent is to create your dream job, you need to sit down and envision that dream job. If you require an education to acquire this dream job then it is up to you to educate yourself. Education comes in many ways.

In the beginning, you will most likely receive your intention through your teacher, either in class situations, blogs, or videos. Your job is to muscle test:

- Is this intent 100% true?

- Is this intent complete?

- Does this intent align to my Divine Heart Crystal?
  (Your Divine Diamond Heart Crystal is an etheric crystal that holds the vibration of your true essence self.)

- Does this intent align to my Divine Purpose?

- Does this intent align to my Divine Soul's Contract of Divine Love and Divine Light?

- Does this intent align to the heart of my Divine Twin Flame?

- Does this intent align to all Cosmic Law?

- Does this intent align to the Divine Oneness of Divine Love and Divine Light?

- Is my protocol complete?

- Do I have full permission for this intent?

If you get a *yes* to every question, state the following:

> **"It is my intent to align my Divine Diamond Heart Crystal to this intent now!**
> **Thank you! Thank you! Thank you!"**

Two Diamond Hearts

Chapter 5: How to Tone

Tones come from our heart. They don't require musical training. Everyone embodies a tone, which is required for Sonic Reiki. However, many people have blocks which inhibit their tone. The work of Sonic Reiki is to free ourselves to do toning. The sound is accessed by our intent for purity, clarity and innocence. That's why some of our tones can sound childlike while others sound ancient or ancestral.

When we tone we tone from our hearts. It is important that we tone at least two syllables and use more vowel sounds than consonants.

Holy men of primitive societies of the world use a spirit language to communicate with higher consciousness for healing purposes. Going back to the 6th century, Pythagoras acknowledged the healing powers of the human voice. He treated disease patterns by reading poetry to his patients. He taught his students how to use their voices to restore balance to their body and soul.

A Sonic Reiki practitioner is taught how to create a scalar wave with his/her voice. Instant healing can take place when a scalar wave pattern with an intent for healing comes from the heart of the practitioner and matches the intensity of the vibration of a client's disease pattern.

Sit or stand in a comfortable position. Take a slow deep breath from your abdomen and let the tones sound from your heart. Allow it to flow without judgment for as long as it feels right. Closing your eyes will help you feel your body as you tone. Edgar Cayce said that sound will be the medicine of the future.

Muscle test this: "Is the future he was talking about *now*?"

Chapter 6: What is a Quantum Configuration Chamber?

Quantum Configuration Chamber

SOUND CODES

SOUND CODES

LIGHT CODES

A SPACE WITHIN
A Space Where There is No Time

SONIC REIKI™

The Quantum Configuration Chamber is one of the universe's greatest gifts of the 21st century. It is a unique tool accessed through Sonic Reiki because of the use of sound and colors.

An individual and/or practitioner uses intent and an elaborate protocol easily and effortlessly, as energy follows intent.

A Quantum Configuration Chamber is a cylinder or bubble which consists of a mesh of interwoven color and sound, creating a space within a space where there is no time. With intent and sound, it can be created to surround a person and/or a specific part of the body. In this space, a Sonic Reiki practitioner using intent can go back to the point within the cellular memory before a trauma occurred. This is a great way to easily and effortlessly release the energy of emotions from sexual abuse, post traumatic stress disorder, or painful childhood experiences. One would still have the memory of the experience without the emotional charge of it.

There are many different kinds of chambers used in Sonic Reiki. Those most commonly utilized are those which are used for protection, to release negative energies such as entities and chambers for manifesting. We also have chambers to repair DNA/RNA, to repair cell damage, for healing different systems such as the nervous system.

Watercolor by Thomas Burakowski

Russian scientists have studied sound's effect on DNA for years. They've learned that DNA can memorize information, and that our genetic code resembles verbal communication.

In Sonic Reiki, a practitioner uses a light language. This spiritual language awakens what the scientists refer to as your "junk DNA." Once this process begins, your cellular biology receives a new operating system, which allows us to rejuvenate at a rapid pace once the root cause is addressed.

Healing the Physical Inner Children

Your physical inner children are your 1-year old self, your 2-year old self, your 3-year old self, etc., collectively. For example, if I am 60 years old, I have 60 physical inner children, each having different needs and desires. If I held jealousy in the majority of the collective consciousness of my physical inner children, then jealousy would be a driving force in my life.

By using an intent, color, a quantum configuration chamber and sound one can easily release or transmute the negative energies in your driver's seat of life.

Included in this book are almost 100 different physical inner children intents for you to choose from. Sit in meditation or muscle test to see which intent is your primary intent. Sometimes you might **think** an intent is important, while, in fact, your physical body is telling you something different. This happens when we suppress our feelings. In the beginning, do only one or two intents a day, as some people become tired as they release. As the parent of your physical inner children, you should nurture yourself during this time (see page 115).

If you are looking for a specific intent and you don't see it in this book, e-mail *soundmaster55@verizon.net* to have one written up for you.

Chapter 7: Physical Inner Children Intents

"Releasing Jealousy"

It is my intent to create a Quantum Configuration Chamber of 777314697 to the power of 4. It is also my intent, using the Divine Colors of Liquid Platinum Yellow and Liquid Pearl Essence, to transmute the frequency of jealousy within my collective consciousness of physical inner children, in all dimensions, in all harmonic universes, in all galaxies and in all cubes now. I ask Lady Grace to grace any and all karma in regards to this intent. I also ask the heart of my Twin Flame, Lady Liberty, Lady Justice and the heart of my physical inner children for full permission for the highest possible reality now!

Muscle test the following:

Is this intent complete?

Does this intent align to Divine Truth?

Is my protocol complete?

Do I have full permission for this intent now?

If so, say the following: "It is my intent to align my Divine Diamond Heart Crystal to this intent now."

Thank you! Thank you! Thank you!

Tone from your heart with all its glory!

And so it is!

Chapter 7: Physical Inner Children Intents

"Releasing Grief"

It is my intent to create a Quantum Configuration Chamber of 792333794 to the power of 6. It is also my intent, using the Divine Colors of Liquid Emerald Green and Liquid Silvery Blue, to transmute the frequency of grief within my collective consciousness of physical inner children, in all dimensions, in all harmonic universes, in all galaxies and in all cubes now. I ask Lady Grace to grace any and all karma in regards to this intent. I also ask the heart of my Twin Flame, Lady Liberty, Lady Justice and the heart of my physical inner children for full permission for the highest possible reality now!

Muscle test the following:

Is this intent complete?

Does this intent align to Divine Truth?

Is my protocol complete?

Do I have full permission for this intent now?

If so, say the following: "It is my intent to align my Divine Diamond Heart Crystal to this intent now."

Thank you! Thank you! Thank you!

Tone from your heart with all its glory!

And so it is!

Chapter 7: Physical Inner Children Intents

"Releasing Denial"

It is my intent to create a Quantum Configuration Chamber of 996843895 to the power of 3. It is also my intent, using the Divine Colors of Liquid Blue Diamond and Liquid Orange, to transmute the frequency of denial within my collective consciousness of physical inner children, in all dimensions, in all harmonic universes, in all galaxies and in all cubes now. I ask Lady Grace to grace any and all karma in regards to this intent. I also ask the heart of my Twin Flame, Lady Liberty, Lady Justice and the heart of my physical inner children for full permission for the highest possible reality now!

Muscle test the following:

Is this intent complete?

Does this intent align to Divine Truth?

Is my protocol complete?

Do I have full permission for this intent now?

If so, say the following: "It is my intent to align my Divine Diamond Heart Crystal to this intent now."

Thank you! Thank you! Thank you!

Tone from your heart with all its glory!

And so it is!

Chapter 7: Physical Inner Children Intents

"Releasing Hatred"

It is my intent to create a Quantum Configuration Chamber of 207856491 to the power of 2. It is also my intent, using the Divine Colors of Metallic Green and Liquid Gold, to transmute the frequency of hatred within my collective consciousness of physical inner children, in all dimensions, in all harmonic universes, in all galaxies and in all cubes now. I ask Lady Grace to grace any and all karma in regards to this intent. I also ask the heart of my Twin Flame, Lady Liberty, Lady Justice and the heart of my physical inner children for full permission for the highest possible reality now!

Muscle test the following:

Is this intent complete?

Does this intent align to Divine Truth?

Is my protocol complete?

Do I have full permission for this intent now?

If so, say the following: "It is my intent to align my Divine Diamond Heart Crystal to this intent now."

Thank you! Thank you! Thank you!

Tone from your heart with all its glory!

And so it is!

Chapter 7: Physical Inner Children Intents

"Releasing Loneliness"

It is my intent to create a Quantum Configuration Chamber of 121966747 to the power of 7. It is also my intent, using the Divine Colors of Liquid Yellow and Diamond Pink, to transmute the frequency of loneliness within my collective consciousness of physical inner children, in all dimensions, in all harmonic universes, in all galaxies and in all cubes now. I ask Lady Grace to grace any and all karma in regards to this intent. I also ask the heart of my Twin Flame, Lady Liberty, Lady Justice and the heart of my physical inner children for full permission for the highest possible reality now!

Muscle test the following:

Is this intent complete?

Does this intent align to Divine Truth?

Is my protocol complete?

Do I have full permission for this intent now?

If so, say the following: "It is my intent to align my Divine Diamond Heart Crystal to this intent now."

Thank you! Thank you! Thank you!

Tone from your heart with all its glory!

And so it is!

Chapter 7: Physical Inner Children Intents

"Releasing Anxiety"

It is my intent to create a Quantum Configuration Chamber of 888767888 to the power of 8. It is also my intent, using the Divine Colors of Liquid Royal Blue and White Metallic Powder, to transmute the frequency of anxiety within my collective consciousness of physical inner children, in all dimensions, in all harmonic universes, in all galaxies and in all cubes now. I ask Lady Grace to grace any and all karma in regards to this intent. I also ask the heart of my Twin Flame, Lady Liberty, Lady Justice and the heart of my physical inner children for full permission for the highest possible reality now!

Muscle test the following:

Is this intent complete?

Does this intent align to Divine Truth?

Is my protocol complete?

Do I have full permission for this intent now?

If so, say the following: "It is my intent to align my Divine Diamond Heart Crystal to this intent now."

Thank you! Thank you! Thank you!

Tone from your heart with all its glory!

And so it is!

Chapter 7: Physical Inner Children Intents

"Releasing Sadness"

It is my intent to create a Quantum Configuration Chamber of 994473841 to the power of 3. It is also my intent, using the Divine Colors of Rose and Liquid Lilac, to transmute the frequency of sadness within my collective consciousness of physical inner children, in all dimensions, in all harmonic universes, in all galaxies and in all cubes now. I ask Lady Grace to grace any and all karma in regards to this intent. I also ask the heart of my Twin Flame, Lady Liberty, Lady Justice and the heart of my physical inner children for full permission for the highest possible reality now!

Muscle test the following:

Is this intent complete?

Does this intent align to Divine Truth?

Is my protocol complete?

Do I have full permission for this intent now?

If so, say the following: "It is my intent to align my Divine Diamond Heart Crystal to this intent now."

Thank you! Thank you! Thank you!

Tone from your heart with all its glory!

And so it is!

Chapter 7: Physical Inner Children Intents

"Releasing the Fear of Being Separated from Mother"

It is my intent to create a Quantum Configuration Chamber of 777777777 to the power of 1111111. It is also my intent, using the Divine Colors of Metallic Lavender and Liquid Violet, to transmute the frequency of the fear of being separated from mother within my collective consciousness of physical inner children, in all dimensions, in all harmonic universes, in all galaxies and in all cubes now. I ask Lady Grace to grace any and all karma in regards to this intent. I also ask the heart of my Twin Flame, Lady Liberty, Lady Justice and the heart of my physical inner children for permission for the highest possible reality now!

Muscle test the following:

Is this intent complete?

Does this intent align to Divine Truth?

Is my protocol complete?

Do I have full permission for this intent now?

If so, say the following: "It is my intent to align my Divine Diamond Heart Crystal to this intent now."

Thank you! Thank you! Thank you!

Tone from your heart with all its glory!

And so it is!

Chapter 7: Physical Inner Children Intents

"Releasing the Fear of Being Separated From Father"

It is my intent to create a Quantum Configuration Chamber of 887887887 to the power of 1111111. It is also my intent, using the Divine Colors of Metallic Plum and Opalescent Pink, to transmute the frequency of the fear of being separated from father within my collective consciousness of physical inner children, in all dimensions, in all harmonic universes, in all galaxies and in all cubes now. I ask Lady Grace to grace any and all karma in regards to this intent. I also ask the heart of my Twin Flame, Lady Liberty, Lady Justice and the heart of my physical inner children for permission for the highest possible reality now!

Muscle test the following:

Is this intent complete?

Does this intent align to Divine Truth?

Is my protocol complete?

Do I have full permission for this intent now?

If so, say the following: "It is my intent to align my Divine Diamond Heart Crystal to this intent now."

Thank you! Thank you! Thank you!

Tone from your heart with all its glory!

And so it is!

Chapter 7: Physical Inner Children Intents

"Releasing the Fear of Being Separated from Parents"

It is my intent to create a Quantum Configuration Chamber of 888888888 to the power of 1111111. It is also my intent, using the Divine Colors of Liquid Diamond Rose, to transmute the frequency of the fear of being separated from parents within my collective consciousness of physical inner children, in all dimensions, in all harmonic universes, in all galaxies and in all cubes now. I ask Lady Grace to grace any and all karma in regards to this intent. I also ask the heart of my Twin Flame, Lady Liberty, Lady Justice and the heart of my physical inner children for permission for the highest possible reality now!

Muscle test the following:

Is this intent complete?

Does this intent align to Divine Truth?

Is my protocol complete?

Do I have full permission for this intent now?

If so, say the following: "It is my intent to align my Divine Diamond Heart Crystal to this intent now."

Thank you! Thank you! Thank you!

Tone from your heart with all its glory!

And so it is!

Chapter 7: Physical Inner Children Intents

"Releasing Naivety"

It is my intent to create a Quantum Configuration Chamber of 555767484 to the power of 4. It is also my intent, using the Divine Colors of Liquid Green Violet and Metallic Rose, to transmute the frequency of naivety within my collective consciousness of physical inner children, in all dimensions, in all harmonic universes, in all galaxies and in all cubes now. I ask Lady Grace to grace any and all karma in regards to this intent. I also ask the heart of my Twin Flame, Lady Liberty, Lady Justice and the heart of my physical inner children for permission for the highest possible reality now!

Muscle test the following:

Is this intent complete?

Does this intent align to Divine Truth?

Is my protocol complete?

Do I have full permission for this intent now?

If so, say the following: "It is my intent to align my Divine Diamond Heart Crystal to this intent now."

Thank you! Thank you! Thank you!

Tone from your heart with all its glory!

And so it is!

Chapter 7: Physical Inner Children Intents

"Releasing Helplessness"

It is my intent to create a Quantum Configuration Chamber of 555978555 to the power of 5. It is also my intent, using the Divine Colors of Metallic Violet and Liquid Yellow, to transmute the frequency of helplessness within my collective consciousness of physical inner children, in all dimensions, in all harmonic universes, in all galaxies and in all cubes now. I ask Lady Grace to grace any and all karma in regards to this intent. I also ask the heart of my Twin Flame, Lady Liberty, Lady Justice and the heart of my physical inner children for permission for the highest possible reality now!

Muscle test the following:

Is this intent complete?

Does this intent align to Divine Truth?

Is my protocol complete?

Do I have full permission for this intent now?

If so, say the following: "It is my intent to align my Divine Diamond Heart Crystal to this intent now."

Thank you! Thank you! Thank you!

Tone from your heart with all its glory!

And so it is!

Chapter 7: Physical Inner Children Intents

"Releasing Anger"

It is my intent to create a Quantum Configuration Chamber of 666999666 to the power of 5. It is also my intent, using the Divine Colors of Sea Foam Green and Liquid Salmon, to transmute the frequency of anger within my collective consciousness of physical inner children, in all dimensions, in all harmonic universes, in all galaxies and in all cubes now. I ask Lady Grace to grace any and all karma in regards to this intent. I also ask the heart of my Twin Flame, Lady Liberty, Lady Justice and the heart of my physical inner children for permission for the highest possible reality now!

Muscle test the following:

Is this intent complete?

Does this intent align to Divine Truth?

Is my protocol complete?

Do I have full permission for this intent now?

If so, say the following: "It is my intent to align my Divine Diamond Heart Crystal to this intent now."

Thank you! Thank you! Thank you!

Tone from your heart with all its glory!

And so it is!

Chapter 7: Physical Inner Children Intents

"Releasing Resentment"

It is my intent to create a Quantum Configuration Chamber of 999878945 to the power of 3. It is also my intent, using the Divine Colors of Lavender and Liquid Violet, to transmute the frequency of resentment within my collective consciousness of physical inner children, in all dimensions, in all harmonic universes, in all galaxies and in all cubes now. I ask Lady Grace to grace any and all karma in regards to this intent. I also ask the heart of my Twin Flame, Lady Liberty, Lady Justice and the heart of my physical inner children for permission for the highest possible reality now!

Muscle test the following:

Is this intent complete?

Does this intent align to Divine Truth?

Is my protocol complete?

Do I have full permission for this intent now?

If so, say the following: "It is my intent to align my Divine Diamond Heart Crystal to this intent now."

Thank you! Thank you! Thank you!

Tone from your heart with all its glory!

And so it is!

Chapter 7: Physical Inner Children Intents

"Releasing Guilt"

It is my intent to create a Quantum Configuration Chamber of 999797959 to the power of 3. It is also my intent, using the Divine Colors of Metallic Violet and Liquid Turquoise, to transmute the frequency of guilt within my collective consciousness of physical inner children, in all dimensions, in all harmonic universes, in all galaxies and in all cubes now. I ask Lady Grace to grace any and all karma in regards to this intent. I also ask the heart of my Twin Flame, Lady Liberty, Lady Justice and the heart of my physical inner children for permission for the highest possible reality now!

Muscle test the following:

Is this intent complete?

Does this intent align to Divine Truth?

Is my protocol complete?

Do I have full permission for this intent now?

If so, say the following: "It is my intent to align my Divine Diamond Heart Crystal to this intent now."

Thank you! Thank you! Thank you!

Tone from your heart with all its glory!

And so it is!

Chapter 7: Physical Inner Children Intents

"Releasing Passiveness"

It is my intent to create a Quantum Configuration Chamber of 999454999 to the power of 6. It is also my intent, using the Divine Colors of Metallic Yellow and Liquid Emerald Green, to transmute the frequency of passiveness within my collective consciousness of physical inner children, in all dimensions, in all harmonic universes, in all galaxies and in all cubes now. I ask Lady Grace to grace any and all karma in regards to this intent. I also ask the heart of my Twin Flame, Lady Liberty, Lady Justice and the heart of my physical inner children for permission for the highest possible reality now!

Muscle test the following:

Is this intent complete?

Does this intent align to Divine Truth?

Is my protocol complete?

Do I have full permission for this intent now?

If so, say the following: "It is my intent to align my Divine Diamond Heart Crystal to this intent now."

Thank you! Thank you! Thank you!

Tone from your heart with all its glory!

And so it is!

Chapter 7: Physical Inner Children Intents

"Releasing Aggressiveness"

It is my intent to create a Quantum Configuration Chamber of 999474393 to the power of 3. It is also my intent, using the Divine Colors of Emerald Green and Liquid Yellow, to transmute the frequency of aggressiveness within my collective consciousness of physical inner children, in all dimensions, in all harmonic universes, in all galaxies and in all cubes now. I ask Lady Grace to grace any and all karma in regards to this intent. I also ask the heart of my Twin Flame, Lady Liberty, Lady Justice and the heart of my physical inner children for permission for the highest possible reality now!

Muscle test the following:

Is this intent complete?

Does this intent align to Divine Truth?

Is my protocol complete?

Do I have full permission for this intent now?

If so, say the following: "It is my intent to align my Divine Diamond Heart Crystal to this intent now."

Thank you! Thank you! Thank you!

Tone from your heart with all its glory!

And so it is!

Chapter 7: Physical Inner Children Intents

"Releasing Procrastination"

It is my intent to create a Quantum Configuration Chamber of 999333393 to the power of 3. It is also my intent, using the Divine Colors of Liquid Orange and Metallic Navy Blue, to transmute the frequency of procrastination within my collective consciousness of physical inner children, in all dimensions, in all harmonic universes, in all galaxies and in all cubes now. I ask Lady Grace to grace any and all karma in regards to this intent. I also ask the heart of my Twin Flame, Lady Liberty, Lady Justice and the heart of my physical inner children for permission for the highest possible reality now!

Muscle test the following:

Is this intent complete?

Does this intent align to Divine Truth?

Is my protocol complete?

Do I have full permission for this intent now?

If so, say the following: "It is my intent to align my Divine Diamond Heart Crystal to this intent now."

Thank you! Thank you! Thank you!

Tone from your heart with all its glory!

And so it is!

Chapter 7: Physical Inner Children Intents

"Releasing Loss"

It is my intent to create a Quantum Configuration Chamber of 999313239 to the power of 6. It is also my intent, using the Divine Colors of Liquid Peach and Metallic Powdery White, to transmute the frequency of loss within my collective consciousness of physical inner children, in all dimensions, in all harmonic universes, in all galaxies and in all cubes now. I ask Lady Grace to grace any and all karma in regards to this intent. I also ask the heart of my Twin Flame, Lady Liberty, Lady Justice and the heart of my physical inner children for permission for the highest possible reality now!

Muscle test the following:

Is this intent complete?

Does this intent align to Divine Truth?

Is my protocol complete?

Do I have full permission for this intent now?

If so, say the following: "It is my intent to align my Divine Diamond Heart Crystal to this intent now."

Thank you! Thank you! Thank you!

Tone from your heart with all its glory!

And so it is!

Chapter 7: Physical Inner Children Intents

"Releasing Abandonment"

It is my intent to create a Quantum Configuration Chamber of 999333339 to the power of 6. It is also my intent, using the Divine Colors of Diamond Blue Crystal and Metallic Lemon, to transmute the frequency of abandonment within my collective consciousness of physical inner children, in all dimensions, in all harmonic universes, in all galaxies and in all cubes now. I ask Lady Grace to grace any and all karma in regards to this intent. I also ask the heart of my Twin Flame, Lady Liberty, Lady Justice and the heart of my physical inner children for permission for the highest possible reality now!

Muscle test the following:

Is this intent complete?

Does this intent align to Divine Truth?

Is my protocol complete?

Do I have full permission for this intent now?

If so, say the following: "It is my intent to align my Divine Diamond Heart Crystal to this intent now."

Thank you! Thank you! Thank you!

Tone from your heart with all its glory!

And so it is!

Chapter 7: Physical Inner Children Intents

"Releasing Lack of Discernment"

It is my intent to create a Quantum Configuration Chamber of 999555999 to the power of 3. It is also my intent, using the Divine Colors of Diamond Yellow Crystal and Liquid Peach, to transmute the frequency of lack of discernment within my collective consciousness of physical inner children, in all dimensions, in all harmonic universes, in all galaxies and in all cubes now. I ask Lady Grace to grace any and all karma in regards to this intent. I also ask the heart of my Twin Flame, Lady Liberty, Lady Justice and the heart of my physical inner children for permission for the highest possible reality now!

Muscle test the following:

Is this intent complete?

Does this intent align to Divine Truth?

Is my protocol complete?

Do I have full permission for this intent now?

If so, say the following: "It is my intent to align my Divine Diamond Heart Crystal to this intent now."

Thank you! Thank you! Thank you!

Tone from your heart with all its glory!

And so it is!

Chapter 7: Physical Inner Children Intents

"Releasing Reluctance"

It is my intent to create a Quantum Configuration Chamber of 997444321 to the power of 4. It is also my intent, using the Divine Colors of Metallic Marigold Yellow and Liquid Orange, to transmute the frequency of reluctance within my collective consciousness of physical inner children, in all dimensions, in all harmonic universes, in all galaxies and in all cubes now. I ask Lady Grace to grace any and all karma in regards to this intent. I also ask the heart of my Twin Flame, Lady Liberty, Lady Justice and the heart of my physical inner children for permission for the highest possible reality now!

Muscle test the following:

Is this intent complete?

Does this intent align to Divine Truth?

Is my protocol complete?

Do I have full permission for this intent now?

If so, say the following: "It is my intent to align my Divine Diamond Heart Crystal to this intent now."

Thank you! Thank you! Thank you!

Tone from your heart with all its glory!

And so it is!

Chapter 7: Physical Inner Children Intents

"Releasing the Fear of Being Alone"

It is my intent to create a Quantum Configuration Chamber of 911333979 to the power of 7. It is also my intent, using the Divine Colors of Metallic Creamy Orange and Liquid Yellow, to transmute the frequency of the fear of being alone within my collective consciousness of physical inner children, in all dimensions, in all harmonic universes, in all galaxies and in all cubes now. I ask Lady Grace to grace any and all karma in regards to this intent. I also ask the heart of my Twin Flame, Lady Liberty, Lady Justice and the heart of my physical inner children for permission for the highest possible reality now!

Muscle test the following:

Is this intent complete?

Does this intent align to Divine Truth?

Is my protocol complete?

Do I have full permission for this intent now?

If so, say the following: "It is my intent to align my Divine Diamond Heart Crystal to this intent now."

Thank you! Thank you! Thank you!

Tone from your heart with all its glory!

And so it is!

Chapter 7: Physical Inner Children Intents

"Releasing Poverty Consciousness"

It is my intent to create a Quantum Configuration Chamber of 997799899 to the power of 3. It is also my intent, using the Divine Colors of Metallic Green and Crystalline Purple, to transmute the frequency of poverty consciousness within my collective consciousness of physical inner children, in all dimensions, in all harmonic universes, in all galaxies and in all cubes now. I ask Lady Grace to grace any and all karma in regards to this intent. I also ask the heart of my Twin Flame, Lady Liberty, Lady Justice and the heart of my physical inner children for permission for the highest possible reality now!

Muscle test the following:

Is this intent complete?

Does this intent align to Divine Truth?

Is my protocol complete?

Do I have full permission for this intent now?

If so, say the following: "It is my intent to align my Divine Diamond Heart Crystal to this intent now."

Thank you! Thank you! Thank you!

Tone from your heart with all its glory!

And so it is!

Chapter 7: Physical Inner Children Intents

"Releasing Needing Approval of Others"

It is my intent to create a Quantum Configuration Chamber of 998888899 to the power of 7. It is also my intent, using the Divine Colors of Liquid Yellow and Crystalline Lavender, to transmute the frequency of needing approval of others within my collective consciousness of physical inner children, in all dimensions, in all harmonic universes, in all galaxies and in all cubes now. I ask Lady Grace to grace any and all karma in regards to this intent. I also ask the heart of my Twin Flame, Lady Liberty, Lady Justice and the heart of my physical inner children for permission for the highest possible reality now!

Muscle test the following:

Is this intent complete?

Does this intent align to Divine Truth?

Is my protocol complete?

Do I have full permission for this intent now?

If so, say the following: "It is my intent to align my Divine Diamond Heart Crystal to this intent now."

Thank you! Thank you! Thank you!

Tone from your heart with all its glory!

And so it is!

Chapter 7: Physical Inner Children Intents

"Releasing Low Self Esteem"

It is my intent to create a Quantum Configuration Chamber of 998777899 to the power of 7. It is also my intent, using the Divine Colors of Liquid Lavender and Diamond Blue, to transmute the frequency of low self esteem within my collective consciousness of physical inner children, in all dimensions, in all harmonic universes, in all galaxies and in all cubes now. I ask Lady Grace to grace any and all karma in regards to this intent. I also ask the heart of my Twin Flame, Lady Liberty, Lady Justice and the heart of my physical inner children for permission for the highest possible reality now!

Muscle test the following:

Is this intent complete?

Does this intent align to Divine Truth?

Is my protocol complete?

Do I have full permission for this intent now?

If so, say the following: "It is my intent to align my Divine Diamond Heart Crystal to this intent now."

Thank you! Thank you! Thank you!

Tone from your heart with all its glory!

And so it is!

Chapter 7: Physical Inner Children Intents

"Releasing Low Self Worth"

It is my intent to create a Quantum Configuration Chamber of 996666699 to the power of 6. It is also my intent, using the Divine Colors of Metallic Red and Crystalline Lavender, to transmute the frequency of low self worth within my collective consciousness of physical inner children, in all dimensions, in all harmonic universes, in all galaxies and in all cubes now. I ask Lady Grace to grace any and all karma in regards to this intent. I also ask the heart of my Twin Flame, Lady Liberty and Lady Justice and the heart of my physical inner children for permission for the highest possible reality now!

Muscle test the following:

Is this intent complete?

Does this intent align to Divine Truth?

Is my protocol complete?

Do I have full permission for this intent now?

If so, say the following: "It is my intent to align my Divine Diamond Heart Crystal to this intent now."

Thank you! Thank you! Thank you!

Tone from your heart with all its glory!

And so it is!

Chapter 7: Physical Inner Children Intents

"Releasing the Need to Always Please Parents"

It is my intent to create a Quantum Configuration Chamber of 994545646 to the power of 6. It is also my intent, using the Divine Colors of Diamond Pink and Crystalline Gold, to transmute the frequency of the need to always please parents within my collective consciousness of physical inner children, in all dimensions, in all harmonic universes, in all galaxies and in all cubes now. I ask Lady Grace to grace any and all karma in regards to this intent. I also ask the heart of my Twin Flame, Lady Liberty, Lady Justice and the heart of my physical inner children for permission for the highest possible reality now!

Muscle test the following:

Is this intent complete?

Does this intent align to Divine Truth?

Is my protocol complete?

Do I have full permission for this intent now?

If so, say the following: "It is my intent to align my Divine Diamond Heart Crystal to this intent now."

Thank you! Thank you! Thank you!

Tone from your heart with all its glory!

And so it is!

Chapter 7: Physical Inner Children Intents

"Releasing the Energy of Being a Pessimistic"

It is my intent to create a Quantum Configuration Chamber of 999868989 to the power of 3. It is also my intent, using the Divine Colors of Diamond Mauve and Crystalline Forest Green, to transmute the frequency of the energy of being a pessimistic within my collective consciousness of physical inner children, in all dimensions, in all harmonic universes, in all galaxies and in all cubes now. I ask Lady Grace to grace any and all karma in regards to this intent. I also ask the heart of my Twin Flame, Lady Liberty, Lady Justice and the heart of my physical inner children for permission for the highest possible reality now!

Muscle test the following:

Is this intent complete?

Does this intent align to Divine Truth?

Is my protocol complete?

Do I have full permission for this intent now?

If so, say the following: "It is my intent to align my Divine Diamond Heart Crystal to this intent now."

Thank you! Thank you! Thank you!

Tone from your heart with all its glory!

And so it is!

Chapter 7: Physical Inner Children Intents

"Releasing the Making the Wrong Decision"

It is my intent to create a Quantum Configuration Chamber of 999010633 to the power of 4. It is also my intent, using the Divine Colors of Diamond Magenta and Crystalline Gold, to transmute the frequency of making the wrong decision within my collective consciousness of physical inner children, in all dimensions, in all harmonic universes, in all galaxies and in all cubes now. I ask Lady Grace to grace any and all karma in regards to this intent. I also ask the heart of my Twin Flame, Lady Liberty, Lady Justice and the heart of my physical inner children for permission for the highest possible reality now!

Muscle test the following:

Is this intent complete?

Does this intent align to Divine Truth?

Is my protocol complete?

Do I have full permission for this intent now?

If so, say the following: "It is my intent to align my Divine Diamond Heart Crystal to this intent now."

Thank you! Thank you! Thank you!

Tone from your heart with all its glory!

And so it is!

Chapter 7: Physical Inner Children Intents

"Releasing the Lack of Confidence"

It is my intent to create a Quantum Configuration Chamber of 999779689 to the power of 9. It is also my intent, using the Divine Colors of Metallic Yellow and Crystalline Electrifying Blue, to transmute the frequency of lack of confidence within my collective consciousness of physical inner children, in all dimensions, in all harmonic universes, in all galaxies and in all cubes now. I ask Lady Grace to grace any and all karma in regards to this intent. I also ask the heart of my Twin Flame, Lady Liberty, Lady Justice and the heart of my physical inner children for permission for the highest possible reality now!

Muscle test the following:

Is this intent complete?

Does this intent align to Divine Truth?

Is my protocol complete?

Do I have full permission for this intent now?

If so, say the following: "It is my intent to align my Divine Diamond Heart Crystal to this intent now."

Thank you! Thank you! Thank you!

Tone from your heart with all its glory!

And so it is!

Chapter 7: Physical Inner Children Intents

"Releasing Panic"

It is my intent to create a Quantum Configuration Chamber of 998767456 to the power of 6. It is also my intent, using the Divine Colors of Liquid Peach and Crystalline Midnight Blue, to transmute the frequency of panic within my collective consciousness of physical inner children, in all dimensions, in all harmonic universes, in all galaxies and in all cubes now. I ask Lady Grace to grace any and all karma in regards to this intent. I also ask the heart of my Twin Flame, Lady Liberty, Lady Justice and the heart of my physical inner children for permission for the highest possible reality now!

Muscle test the following:

Is this intent complete?

Does this intent align to Divine Truth?

Is my protocol complete?

Do I have full permission for this intent now?

If so, say the following: "It is my intent to align my Divine Diamond Heart Crystal to this intent now."

Thank you! Thank you! Thank you!

Tone from your heart with all its glory!

And so it is!

Chapter 7: Physical Inner Children Intents

"Releasing Being Lost"

It is my intent to create a Quantum Configuration Chamber of 999776443 to the power of 3. It is also my intent, using the Divine Colors of Metallic Yellow/Peach and Diamond Pink, to transmute the frequency of being lost within my collective consciousness of physical inner children, in all dimensions, in all harmonic universes, in all galaxies and in all cubes now. I ask Lady Grace to grace any and all karma in regards to this intent. I also ask the heart of my Twin Flame, Lady Liberty, Lady Justice and the heart of my physical inner children for permission for the highest possible reality now!

Muscle test the following:

Is this intent complete?

Does this intent align to Divine Truth?

Is my protocol complete?

Do I have full permission for this intent now?

If so, say the following: "It is my intent to align my Divine Diamond Heart Crystal to this intent now."

Thank you! Thank you! Thank you!

Tone from your heart with all its glory!

And so it is!

Chapter 7: Physical Inner Children Intents

"Releasing Illusion"

It is my intent to create a Quantum Configuration Chamber of 998888797 to the power of 6. It is also my intent, using the Divine Colors of Crystalline Emerald Green and Metallic Magenta, to transmute the frequency of illusion within my collective consciousness of physical inner children, in all dimensions, in all harmonic universes, in all galaxies and in all cubes now. I ask Lady Grace to grace any and all karma in regards to this intent. I also ask the heart of my Twin Flame, Lady Liberty, Lady Justice and the heart of my physical inner children for permission for the highest possible reality now!

Muscle test the following:

Is this intent complete?

Does this intent align to Divine Truth?

Is my protocol complete?

Do I have full permission for this intent now?

If so, say the following: "It is my intent to align my Divine Diamond Heart Crystal to this intent now."

Thank you! Thank you! Thank you!

Tone from your heart with all its glory!

And so it is!

Chapter 7: Physical Inner Children Intents

"Releasing Embarrassment"

It is my intent to create a Quantum Configuration Chamber of 999797665 to the power of 5. It is also my intent, using the Divine Colors of Diamond Turquoise and Diamond Silver, to transmute the frequency of embarrassment within my collective consciousness of physical inner children, in all dimensions, in all harmonic universes, in all galaxies and in all cubes now. I ask Lady Grace to grace any and all karma in regards to this intent. I also ask the heart of my Twin Flame, Lady Liberty, Lady Justice and the heart of my physical inner children for permission for the highest possible reality now!

Muscle test the following:

Is this intent complete?

Does this intent align to Divine Truth?

Is my protocol complete?

Do I have full permission for this intent now?

If so, say the following: "It is my intent to align my Divine Diamond Heart Crystal to this intent now."

Thank you! Thank you! Thank you!

Tone from your heart with all its glory!

And so it is!

Chapter 7: Physical Inner Children Intents

"Releasing Humiliation"

It is my intent to create a Quantum Configuration Chamber of 997779779 to the power of 7. It is also my intent, using the Divine Colors of Diamond Red and Metallic Orange, to transmute the frequency of humiliation within my collective consciousness of physical inner children, in all dimensions, in all harmonic universes, in all galaxies and in all cubes now. I ask Lady Grace to grace any and all karma in regards to this intent. I also ask the heart of my Twin Flame, Lady Liberty and Lady Justice and the heart of my physical inner children for permission for the highest possible reality now!

Muscle test the following:

Is this intent complete?

Does this intent align to Divine Truth?

Is my protocol complete?

Do I have full permission for this intent now?

If so, say the following: "It is my intent to align my Divine Diamond Heart Crystal to this intent now."

Thank you! Thank you! Thank you!

Tone from your heart with all its glory!

And so it is!

Chapter 7: Physical Inner Children Intents

"Releasing Shame"

It is my intent to create a Quantum Configuration Chamber of 999676888 to the power of 5. It is also my intent, using the Divine Colors of Metallic Violet and Liquid Yellow, to transmute the frequency of shame within my collective consciousness of physical inner children, in all dimensions, in all harmonic universes, in all galaxies and in all cubes now. I ask Lady Grace to grace any and all karma in regards to this intent. I also ask the heart of my Twin Flame, Lady Liberty, Lady Justice and the heart of my physical inner children for permission for the highest possible reality now!

Muscle test the following:

Is this intent complete?

Does this intent align to Divine Truth?

Is my protocol complete?

Do I have full permission for this intent now?

If so, say the following: "It is my intent to align my Divine Diamond Heart Crystal to this intent now."

Thank you! Thank you! Thank you!

Tone from your heart with all its glory!

And so it is!

Chapter 7: Physical Inner Children Intents

"Releasing Stupidity"

It is my intent to create a Quantum Configuration Chamber of 988988777 to the power of 3. It is also my intent, using the Divine Colors of Metallic Maroon and Liquid White, to transmute the frequency of stupidity within my collective consciousness of physical inner children, in all dimensions, in all harmonic universes, in all galaxies and in all cubes now. I ask Lady Grace to grace any and all karma in regards to this intent. I also ask the heart of my Twin Flame, Lady Liberty, Lady Justice and the heart of my physical inner children for permission for the highest possible reality now!

Muscle test the following:

Is this intent complete?

Does this intent align to Divine Truth?

Is my protocol complete?

Do I have full permission for this intent now?

If so, say the following: "It is my intent to align my Divine Diamond Heart Crystal to this intent now."

Thank you! Thank you! Thank you!

Tone from your heart with all its glory!

And so it is!

Chapter 7: Physical Inner Children Intents

"Releasing Rage"

It is my intent to create a Quantum Configuration Chamber of 999595799 to the power of 7. It is also my intent, using the Divine Colors of Diamond Indigo and Liquid Peach, to transmute the frequency of rage within my collective consciousness of physical inner children, in all dimensions, in all harmonic universes, in all galaxies and in all cubes now. I ask Lady Grace to grace any and all karma in regards to this intent. I also ask the heart of my Twin Flame, Lady Liberty, Lady Justice and the heart of my physical inner children for permission for the highest possible reality now!

Muscle test the following:

Is this intent complete?

Does this intent align to Divine Truth?

Is my protocol complete?

Do I have full permission for this intent now?

If so, say the following: "It is my intent to align my Divine Diamond Heart Crystal to this intent now."

Thank you! Thank you! Thank you!

Tone from your heart with all its glory!

And so it is!

Chapter 7: Physical Inner Children Intents

"Releasing the Bully Within"

It is my intent to create a Quantum Configuration Chamber of 999999898 to the power of 8. It is also my intent, using the Divine Colors of Metallic Lime Green and Liquid Rose Wine, to transmute the frequency of the bully within my collective consciousness of physical inner children, in all dimensions, in all harmonic universes, in all galaxies and in all cubes now. I ask Lady Grace to grace any and all karma in regards to this intent. I also ask the heart of my Twin Flame, Lady Liberty, Lady Justice and the heart of my physical inner children for permission for the highest possible reality now!

Muscle test the following:

Is this intent complete?

Does this intent align to Divine Truth?

Is my protocol complete?

Do I have full permission for this intent now?

If so, say the following: "It is my intent to align my Divine Diamond Heart Crystal to this intent now."

Thank you! Thank you! Thank you!

Tone from your heart with all its glory!

And so it is!

Chapter 7: Physical Inner Children Intents

"Releasing the Fear of Someone Close to Me Dying"

It is my intent to create a Quantum Configuration Chamber of 997777898 to the power of 3. It is also my intent, using the Divine Colors of Metallic Forest Green and Liquid Yellow, to transmute the frequency of the fear of someone close to me dying within my collective consciousness of physical inner children, in all dimensions, in all harmonic universes, in all galaxies and in all cubes now. I ask Lady Grace to grace any and all karma in regards to this intent. I also ask the heart of my Twin Flame, Lady Liberty, Lady Justice and the heart of my physical inner children for permission for the highest possible reality now!

Muscle test the following:

Is this intent complete?

Does this intent align to Divine Truth?

Is my protocol complete?

Do I have full permission for this intent now?

If so, say the following: "It is my intent to align my Divine Diamond Heart Crystal to this intent now."

Thank you! Thank you! Thank you!

Tone from your heart with all its glory!

And so it is!

Chapter 7: Physical Inner Children Intents

"Releasing the Fear of Being Shunned"

It is my intent to create a Quantum Configuration Chamber of 998887779 to the power of 8. It is also my intent, using the Divine Colors of Liquid Rose and Metallic Silver, to transmute the frequency of the fear of being shunned within my collective consciousness of physical inner children, in all dimensions, in all harmonic universes, in all galaxies and in all cubes now. I ask Lady Grace to grace any and all karma in regards to this intent. I also ask the heart of my Twin Flame, Lady Liberty, Lady Justice and the heart of my physical inner children for permission for the highest possible reality now!

Muscle test the following:

Is this intent complete?

Does this intent align to Divine Truth?

Is my protocol complete?

Do I have full permission for this intent now?

If so, say the following: "It is my intent to align my Divine Diamond Heart Crystal to this intent now."

Thank you! Thank you! Thank you!

Tone from your heart with all its glory!

And so it is!

Chapter 7: Physical Inner Children Intents

"Releasing the Fear of Failure"

It is my intent to create a Quantum Configuration Chamber of 999998799 to the power of 9. It is also my intent, using the Divine Colors of Metallic Forest Green and Liquid Olive Green, to transmute the frequency of the fear of failure within my collective consciousness of physical inner children, in all dimensions, in all harmonic universes, in all galaxies and in all cubes now. I ask Lady Grace to grace any and all karma in regards to this intent. I also ask the heart of my Twin Flame, Lady Liberty, Lady Justice and the heart of my physical inner children for permission for the highest possible reality now!

Muscle test the following:

Is this intent complete?

Does this intent align to Divine Truth?

Is my protocol complete?

Do I have full permission for this intent now?

If so, say the following: "It is my intent to align my Divine Diamond Heart Crystal to this intent now."

Thank you! Thank you! Thank you!

Tone from your heart with all its glory!

And so it is!

Chapter 7: Physical Inner Children Intents

"Releasing the Fear of Being Judged"

It is my intent to create a Quantum Configuration Chamber of 977783999 to the power of 3. It is also my intent, using the Divine Colors of Liquid Crimson and Diamond Cherry, to transmute the frequency of the fear of being judged within my collective consciousness of physical inner children, in all dimensions, in all harmonic universes, in all galaxies and in all cubes now. I ask Lady Grace to grace any and all karma in regards to this intent. I also ask the heart of my Twin Flame, Lady Liberty, Lady Justice and the heart of my physical inner children for permission for the highest possible reality now!

Muscle test the following:

Is this intent complete?

Does this intent align to Divine Truth?

Is my protocol complete?

Do I have full permission for this intent now?

If so, say the following: "It is my intent to align my Divine Diamond Heart Crystal to this intent now."

Thank you! Thank you! Thank you!

Tone from your heart with all its glory!

And so it is!

Chapter 7: Physical Inner Children Intents

"Releasing Anguish"

It is my intent to create a Quantum Configuration Chamber of 995555987 to the power of 5. It is also my intent, using the Divine Colors of Liquid Fluorescent Pink and Diamond Blue, to transmute the frequency of anguish within my collective consciousness of physical inner children, in all dimensions, in all harmonic universes, in all galaxies and in all cubes now. I ask Lady Grace to grace any and all karma in regards to this intent. I also ask the heart of my Twin Flame, Lady Liberty, Lady Justice and the heart of my physical inner children for permission for the highest possible reality now!

Muscle test the following:

Is this intent complete?

Does this intent align to Divine Truth?

Is my protocol complete?

Do I have full permission for this intent now?

If so, say the following: "It is my intent to align my Divine Diamond Heart Crystal to this intent now."

Thank you! Thank you! Thank you!

Tone from your heart with all its glory!

And so it is!

Chapter 7: Physical Inner Children Intents

"Releasing Despair"

It is my intent to create a Quantum Configuration Chamber of 999675675 to the power of 7. It is also my intent, using the Divine Colors of Liquid Yellow Daffodil and Diamond Plum, to transmute the frequency of despair within my collective consciousness of physical inner children, in all dimensions, in all harmonic universes, in all galaxies and in all cubes now. I ask Lady Grace to grace any and all karma in regards to this intent. I also ask the heart of my Twin Flame, Lady Liberty, Lady Justice and the heart of my physical inner children for permission for the highest possible reality now!

Muscle test the following:

Is this intent complete?

Does this intent align to Divine Truth?

Is my protocol complete?

Do I have full permission for this intent now?

If so, say the following: "It is my intent to align my Divine Diamond Heart Crystal to this intent now."

Thank you! Thank you! Thank you!

Tone from your heart with all its glory!

And so it is!

Chapter 7: Physical Inner Children Intents

"Releasing Being Unwanted"

It is my intent to create a Quantum Configuration Chamber of 998994333 to the power of 3. It is also my intent, using the Divine Colors of Liquid Orchid and Diamond Hunter Green, to transmute the frequency of being unwanted within my collective consciousness of physical inner children, in all dimensions, in all harmonic universes, in all galaxies and in all cubes now. I ask Lady Grace to grace any and all karma in regards to this intent. I also ask the heart of my Twin Flame, Lady Liberty, Lady Justice and the heart of my physical inner children for permission for the highest possible reality now!

Muscle test the following:

Is this intent complete?

Does this intent align to Divine Truth?

Is my protocol complete?

Do I have full permission for this intent now?

If so, say the following: "It is my intent to align my Divine Diamond Heart Crystal to this intent now."

Thank you! Thank you! Thank you!

Tone from your heart with all its glory!

And so it is!

Chapter 7: Physical Inner Children Intents

"Releasing Being Overwhelmed"

It is my intent to create a Quantum Configuration Chamber of 993222929 to the power of 3. It is also my intent, using the Divine Colors of Liquid Jungle Green and Diamond Fuchsia, to transmute the frequency of being overwhelmed within my collective consciousness of physical inner children, in all dimensions, in all harmonic universes, in all galaxies and in all cubes now. I ask Lady Grace to grace any and all karma in regards to this intent. I also ask the heart of my Twin Flame, Lady Liberty, Lady Justice and the heart of my physical inner children for permission for the highest possible reality now!

Muscle test the following:

Is this intent complete?

Does this intent align to Divine Truth?

Is my protocol complete?

Do I have full permission for this intent now?

If so, say the following: "It is my intent to align my Divine Diamond Heart Crystal to this intent now."

Thank you! Thank you! Thank you!

Tone from your heart with all its glory!

And so it is!

Chapter 7: Physical Inner Children Intents

"Releasing the Fear of Being Rejected"

It is my intent to create a Quantum Configuration Chamber of 999343999 to the power of 3. It is also my intent, using the Divine Colors of Diamond Orange and Metallic Golden Poppy, to transmute the frequency of the fear of being rejected within my collective consciousness of physical inner children, in all dimensions, in all harmonic universes, in all galaxies and in all cubes now. I ask Lady Grace to grace any and all karma in regards to this intent. I also ask the heart of my Twin Flame, Lady Liberty, Lady Justice and the heart of my physical inner children for permission for the highest possible reality now!

Muscle test the following:

Is this intent complete?

Does this intent align to Divine Truth?

Is my protocol complete?

Do I have full permission for this intent now?

If so, say the following: "It is my intent to align my Divine Diamond Heart Crystal to this intent now."

Thank you! Thank you! Thank you!

Tone from your heart with all its glory!

And so it is!

Chapter 7: Physical Inner Children Intents

"Releasing the Fear of Being Ignored"

It is my intent to create a Quantum Configuration Chamber of 999787088 to the power of 2. It is also my intent, using the Divine Colors of Liquid Cobalt Blue and Metallic Rose, to transmute the frequency of the fear of being ignored within my collective consciousness of physical inner children, in all dimensions, in all harmonic universes, in all galaxies and in all cubes now. I ask Lady Grace to grace any and all karma in regards to this intent. I also ask the heart of my Twin Flame, Lady Liberty, Lady Justice and the heart of my physical inner children for permission for the highest possible reality now!

Muscle test the following:

Is this intent complete?

Does this intent align to Divine Truth?

Is my protocol complete?

Do I have full permission for this intent now?

If so, say the following: "It is my intent to align my Divine Diamond Heart Crystal to this intent now."

Thank you! Thank you! Thank you!

Tone from your heart with all its glory!

And so it is!

Chapter 7: Physical Inner Children Intents

"Releasing the Fear of Being Left Behind"

It is my intent to create a Quantum Configuration Chamber of 999998679 to the power of 6. It is also my intent, using the Divine Colors of Liquid Peach and Metallic Lime Green, to transmute the frequency of the fear of being left behind within my collective consciousness of physical inner children, in all dimensions, in all harmonic universes, in all galaxies and in all cubes now. I ask Lady Grace to grace any and all karma in regards to this intent. I also ask the heart of my Twin Flame, Lady Liberty, Lady Justice and the heart of my physical inner children for permission for the highest possible reality now!

Muscle test the following:

Is this intent complete?

Does this intent align to Divine Truth?

Is my protocol complete?

Do I have full permission for this intent now?

If so, say the following: "It is my intent to align my Divine Diamond Heart Crystal to this intent now."

Thank you! Thank you! Thank you!

Tone from your heart with all its glory!

And so it is!

Chapter 7: Physical Inner Children Intents

"Releasing the Fear of Being Attacked"

It is my intent to create a Quantum Configuration Chamber of 999767989 to the power of 5. It is also my intent, using the Divine Colors of Liquid Maroon and Liquid Yellow, to transmute the frequency of the fear of being attacked within my collective consciousness of physical inner children, in all dimensions, in all harmonic universes, in all galaxies and in all cubes now. I ask Lady Grace to grace any and all karma in regards to this intent. I also ask the heart of my Twin Flame, Lady Liberty, Lady Justice and the heart of my physical inner children for permission for the highest possible reality now!

Muscle test the following:

Is this intent complete?

Does this intent align to Divine Truth?

Is my protocol complete?

Do I have full permission for this intent now?

If so, say the following: "It is my intent to align my Divine Diamond Heart Crystal to this intent now."

Thank you! Thank you! Thank you!

Tone from your heart with all its glory!

And so it is!

Chapter 7: Physical Inner Children Intents

"Releasing the Fear of Being Taken Advantage Of"

It is my intent to create a Quantum Configuration Chamber of 997996676 to the power of 5. It is also my intent, using the Divine Colors of Liquid Yellow and Diamond Sky Blue, to transmute the frequency of the fear of being taken advantage of within my collective consciousness of physical inner children, in all dimensions, in all harmonic universes, in all galaxies and in all cubes now. I ask Lady Grace to grace any and all karma in regards to this intent. I also ask the heart of my Twin Flame, Lady Liberty, Lady Justice and the heart of my physical inner children for permission for the highest possible reality now!

Muscle test the following:

Is this intent complete?

Does this intent align to Divine Truth?

Is my protocol complete?

Do I have full permission for this intent now?

If so, say the following: "It is my intent to align my Divine Diamond Heart Crystal to this intent now."

Thank you! Thank you! Thank you!

Tone from your heart with all its glory!

And so it is!

Chapter 7: Physical Inner Children Intents

"Releasing the Fear of Fire"

It is my intent to create a Quantum Configuration Chamber of 998799555 to the power of 5. It is also my intent, using the Divine Colors of Liquid Gold and Diamond Rose, to transmute the frequency of the fear of fire within my collective consciousness of physical inner children, in all dimensions, in all harmonic universes, in all galaxies and in all cubes now. I ask Lady Grace to grace any and all karma in regards to this intent. I also ask the heart of my Twin Flame, Lady Liberty, Lady Justice and the heart of my physical inner children for permission for the highest possible reality now!

Muscle test the following:

Is this intent complete?

Does this intent align to Divine Truth?

Is my protocol complete?

Do I have full permission for this intent now?

If so, say the following: "It is my intent to align my Divine Diamond Heart Crystal to this intent now."

Thank you! Thank you! Thank you!

Tone from your heart with all its glory!

And so it is!

Chapter 7: Physical Inner Children Intents

"Releasing the Fear of Water"

It is my intent to create a Quantum Configuration Chamber of 998799333 to the power of 3. It is also my intent, using the Divine Colors of Liquid Royal Blue and Diamond Gold, to transmute the frequency of the fear of water within my collective consciousness of physical inner children, in all dimensions, in all harmonic universes, in all galaxies and in all cubes now. I ask Lady Grace to grace any and all karma in regards to this intent. I also ask the heart of my Twin Flame, Lady Liberty, Lady Justice and the heart of my physical inner children for permission for the highest possible reality now!

Muscle test the following:

Is this intent complete?

Does this intent align to Divine Truth?

Is my protocol complete?

Do I have full permission for this intent now?

If so, say the following: "It is my intent to align my Divine Diamond Heart Crystal to this intent now."

Thank you! Thank you! Thank you!

Tone from your heart with all its glory!

And so it is!

Chapter 7: Physical Inner Children Intents

"Releasing the Fear of Heights"

It is my intent to create a Quantum Configuration Chamber of 998799355 to the power of 5. It is also my intent, using the Divine Colors of Liquid Powder Blue and Diamond Cobalt Blue, to transmute the frequency of the fear of heights within my collective consciousness of physical inner children, in all dimensions, in all harmonic universes, in all galaxies and in all cubes now. I ask Lady Grace to grace any and all karma in regards to this intent. I also ask the heart of my Twin Flame, Lady Liberty, Lady Justice and the heart of my physical inner children for permission for the highest possible reality now!

Muscle test the following:

Is this intent complete?

Does this intent align to Divine Truth?

Is my protocol complete?

Do I have full permission for this intent now?

If so, say the following: "It is my intent to align my Divine Diamond Heart Crystal to this intent now."

Thank you! Thank you! Thank you!

Tone from your heart with all its glory!

And so it is!

Chapter 7: Physical Inner Children Intents

"Releasing Self Sabotage"

It is my intent to create a Quantum Configuration Chamber of 999878675 to the power of 7. It is also my intent, using the Divine Colors of Liquid Crimson and Diamond Apricot, to transmute the frequency of self sabotage within my collective consciousness of physical inner children, in all dimensions, in all harmonic universes, in all galaxies and in all cubes now. I ask Lady Grace to grace any and all karma in regards to this intent. I also ask the heart of my Twin Flame, Lady Liberty, Lady Justice and the heart of my physical inner children for permission for the highest possible reality now!

Muscle test the following:

Is this intent complete?

Does this intent align to Divine Truth?

Is my protocol complete?

Do I have full permission for this intent now?

If so, say the following: "It is my intent to align my Divine Diamond Heart Crystal to this intent now."

Thank you! Thank you! Thank you!

Tone from your heart with all its glory!

And so it is!

Chapter 7: Physical Inner Children Intents

"Releasing Codependency"

It is my intent to create a Quantum Configuration Chamber of 999626262 to the power of 2. It is also my intent, using the Divine Colors of Liquid Fuchsia and Diamond Goldenrod Yellow, to transmute the frequency of codependency within my collective consciousness of physical inner children, in all dimensions, in all harmonic universes, in all galaxies and in all cubes now. I ask Lady Grace to grace any and all karma in regards to this intent. I also ask the heart of my Twin Flame, Lady Liberty, Lady Justice and the heart of my physical inner children for permission for the highest possible reality now!

Muscle test the following:

Is this intent complete?

Does this intent align to Divine Truth?

Is my protocol complete?

Do I have full permission for this intent now?

If so, say the following: "It is my intent to align my Divine Diamond Heart Crystal to this intent now."

Thank you! Thank you! Thank you!

Tone from your heart with all its glory!

And so it is!

Chapter 7: Physical Inner Children Intents

"Releasing My False Self"

It is my intent to create a Quantum Configuration Chamber of 996777878 to the power of 8. It is also my intent, using the Divine Colors of Liquid Lapis Lazuli and Diamond Lavender Blue, to transmute the frequency of my false self within my collective consciousness of physical inner children, in all dimensions, in all harmonic universes, in all galaxies and in all cubes now. I ask Lady Grace to grace any and all karma in regards to this intent. I also ask the heart of my Twin Flame, Lady Liberty, Lady Justice and the heart of my physical inner children for permission for the highest possible reality now!

Muscle test the following:

Is this intent complete?

Does this intent align to Divine Truth?

Is my protocol complete?

Do I have full permission for this intent now?

If so, say the following: "It is my intent to align my Divine Diamond Heart Crystal to this intent now."

Thank you! Thank you! Thank you!

Tone from your heart with all its glory!

And so it is!

Chapter 7: Physical Inner Children Intents

"Releasing Suffering"

It is my intent to create a Quantum Configuration Chamber of 977890777 to the power of 8. It is also my intent, using the Divine Colors of Liquid Kelly Green and Diamond Red, to transmute the frequency of suffering within my collective consciousness of physical inner children, in all dimensions, in all harmonic universes, in all galaxies and in all cubes now. I ask Lady Grace to grace any and all karma in regards to this intent. I also ask the heart of my Twin Flame, Lady Liberty, Lady Justice and the heart of my physical inner children for permission for the highest possible reality now!

Muscle test the following:

Is this intent complete?

Does this intent align to Divine Truth?

Is my protocol complete?

Do I have full permission for this intent now?

If so, say the following: "It is my intent to align my Divine Diamond Heart Crystal to this intent now."

Thank you! Thank you! Thank you!

Tone from your heart with all its glory!

And so it is!

Chapter 7: Physical Inner Children Intents

"Releasing Confusion"

It is my intent to create a Quantum Configuration Chamber of 998996959 to the power of 7. It is also my intent, using the Divine Colors of Liquid Jungle Green and Diamond Jade, to transmute the frequency of confusion within my collective consciousness of physical inner children, in all dimensions, in all harmonic universes, in all galaxies and in all cubes now. I ask Lady Grace to grace any and all karma in regards to this intent. I also ask the heart of my Twin Flame, Lady Liberty, Lady Justice and the heart of my physical inner children for permission for the highest possible reality now!

Muscle test the following:

Is this intent complete?

Does this intent align to Divine Truth?

Is my protocol complete?

Do I have full permission for this intent now?

If so, say the following: "It is my intent to align my Divine Diamond Heart Crystal to this intent now."

Thank you! Thank you! Thank you!

Tone from your heart with all its glory!

And so it is!

Chapter 7: Physical Inner Children Intents

"Releasing Emptiness"

It is my intent to create a Quantum Configuration Chamber of 999878657 to the power of 3. It is also my intent, using the Divine Colors of Liquid Iris and Diamond Ivory, to transmute the frequency of emptiness within my collective consciousness of physical inner children, in all dimensions, in all harmonic universes, in all galaxies and in all cubes now. I ask Lady Grace to grace any and all karma in regards to this intent. I also ask the heart of my Twin Flame, Lady Liberty, Lady Justice and the heart of my physical inner children for permission for the highest possible reality now!

Muscle test the following:

Is this intent complete?

Does this intent align to Divine Truth?

Is my protocol complete?

Do I have full permission for this intent now?

If so, say the following: "It is my intent to align my Divine Diamond Heart Crystal to this intent now."

Thank you! Thank you! Thank you!

Tone from your heart with all its glory!

And so it is!

Chapter 7: Physical Inner Children Intents

"Releasing Unhappiness"

It is my intent to create a Quantum Configuration Chamber of 998997636 to the power of 6. It is also my intent, using the Divine Colors of Liquid Imperial Blue and Diamond Hunter Green, to transmute the frequency of unhappiness within my collective consciousness of physical inner children, in all dimensions, in all harmonic universes, in all galaxies and in all cubes now. I ask Lady Grace to grace any and all karma in regards to this intent. I also ask the heart of my Twin Flame, Lady Liberty, Lady Justice and the heart of my physical inner children for permission for the highest possible reality now!

Muscle test the following:

Is this intent complete?

Does this intent align to Divine Truth?

Is my protocol complete?

Do I have full permission for this intent now?

If so, say the following: "It is my intent to align my Divine Diamond Heart Crystal to this intent now."

Thank you! Thank you! Thank you!

Tone from your heart with all its glory!

And so it is!

Chapter 7: Physical Inner Children Intents

"Releasing Stubbornness"

It is my intent to create a Quantum Configuration Chamber of 987888888 to the power of 8. It is also my intent, using the Divine Colors of Liquid Heliotrope and Diamond Gold, to transmute the frequency of stubbornness within my collective consciousness of physical inner children, in all dimensions, in all harmonic universes, in all galaxies and in all cubes now. I ask Lady Grace to grace any and all karma in regards to this intent. I also ask the heart of my Twin Flame, Lady Liberty, Lady Justice and the heart of my physical inner children for permission for the highest possible reality now!

Muscle test the following:

Is this intent complete?

Does this intent align to Divine Truth?

Is my protocol complete?

Do I have full permission for this intent now?

If so, say the following: "It is my intent to align my Divine Diamond Heart Crystal to this intent now."

Thank you! Thank you! Thank you!

Tone from your heart with all its glory!

And so it is!

Chapter 7: Physical Inner Children Intents

"Releasing Illness"

It is my intent to create a Quantum Configuration Chamber of 977885648 to the power of 6. It is also my intent, using the Divine Colors of Liquid Golden Poppy and Diamond Glaucous, to transmute the frequency of illness within my collective consciousness of physical inner children, in all dimensions, in all harmonic universes, in all galaxies and in all cubes now. I ask Lady Grace to grace any and all karma in regards to this intent. I also ask the heart of my Twin Flame, Lady Liberty, Lady Justice and the heart of my physical inner children for permission for the highest possible reality now!

Muscle test the following:

Is this intent complete?

Does this intent align to Divine Truth?

Is my protocol complete?

Do I have full permission for this intent now?

If so, say the following: "It is my intent to align my Divine Diamond Heart Crystal to this intent now."

Thank you! Thank you! Thank you!

Tone from your heart with all its glory!

And so it is!

Chapter 7: Physical Inner Children Intents

"Releasing Rigidity"

It is my intent to create a Quantum Configuration Chamber of 966565666 to the power of 3. It is also my intent, using the Divine Colors of Liquid Fluorescent Pink and Diamond Beige, to transmute the frequency of rigidity within my collective consciousness of physical inner children, in all dimensions, in all harmonic universes, in all galaxies and in all cubes now. I ask Lady Grace to grace any and all karma in regards to this intent. I also ask the heart of my Twin Flame, Lady Liberty, Lady Justice and the heart of my physical inner children for permission for the highest possible reality now!

Muscle test the following:

Is this intent complete?

Does this intent align to Divine Truth?

Is my protocol complete?

Do I have full permission for this intent now?

If so, say the following: "It is my intent to align my Divine Diamond Heart Crystal to this intent now."

Thank you! Thank you! Thank you!

Tone from your heart with all its glory!

And so it is!

Chapter 7: Physical Inner Children Intents

"Releasing Being Emotionally Cold"

It is my intent to create a Quantum Configuration Chamber of 955878999 to the power of 9. It is also my intent, using the Divine Colors of Liquid Rose and Diamond Lime Green, to transmute the frequency of being emotionally cold within my collective consciousness of physical inner children, in all dimensions, in all harmonic universes, in all galaxies and in all cubes now. I ask Lady Grace to grace any and all karma in regards to this intent. I also ask the heart of my Twin Flame, Lady Liberty, Lady Justice and the heart of my physical inner children for permission for the highest possible reality now!

Muscle test the following:

Is this intent complete?

Does this intent align to Divine Truth?

Is my protocol complete?

Do I have full permission for this intent now?

If so, say the following: "It is my intent to align my Divine Diamond Heart Crystal to this intent now."

Thank you! Thank you! Thank you!

Tone from your heart with all its glory!

And so it is!

Chapter 7: Physical Inner Children Intents

"Releasing Lack of Nurturing"

It is my intent to create a Quantum Configuration Chamber of 977444889 to the power of 4. It is also my intent, using the Divine Colors of Liquid Forest Green and Diamond Pink, to transmute the frequency of lack of nurturing within my collective consciousness of physical inner children, in all dimensions, in all harmonic universes, in all galaxies and in all cubes now. I ask Lady Grace to grace any and all karma in regards to this intent. I also ask the heart of my Twin Flame, Lady Liberty, Lady Justice and the heart of my physical inner children for permission for the highest possible reality now!

Muscle test the following:

Is this intent complete?

Does this intent align to Divine Truth?

Is my protocol complete?

Do I have full permission for this intent now?

If so, say the following: "It is my intent to align my Divine Diamond Heart Crystal to this intent now."

Thank you! Thank you! Thank you!

Tone from your heart with all its glory!

And so it is!

Chapter 7: Physical Inner Children Intents

"Releasing Bondage"

It is my intent to create a Quantum Configuration Chamber of 999787999 to the power of 5. It is also my intent, using the Divine Colors of Liquid Electric Cyan and Diamond Deep Pink, to transmute the frequency of bondage within my collective consciousness of physical inner children, in all dimensions, in all harmonic universes, in all galaxies and in all cubes now. I ask Lady Grace to grace any and all karma in regards to this intent. I also ask the heart of my Twin Flame, Lady Liberty, Lady Justice and the heart of my physical inner children for permission for the highest possible reality now!

Muscle test the following:

Is this intent complete?

Does this intent align to Divine Truth?

Is my protocol complete?

Do I have full permission for this intent now?

If so, say the following: "It is my intent to align my Divine Diamond Heart Crystal to this intent now."

Thank you! Thank you! Thank you!

Tone from your heart with all its glory!

And so it is!

Chapter 7: Physical Inner Children Intents

"Releasing Neglect"

It is my intent to create a Quantum Configuration Chamber of 999999999 to the power of 7. It is also my intent, using the Divine Colors of Liquid Sky Blue and Diamond Dogwood Rose, to transmute the frequency of neglect within my collective consciousness of physical inner children, in all dimensions, in all harmonic universes, in all galaxies and in all cubes now. I ask Lady Grace to grace any and all karma in regards to this intent. I also ask the heart of my Twin Flame, Lady Liberty, Lady Justice and the heart of my physical inner children for permission for the highest possible reality now!

Muscle test the following:

Is this intent complete?

Does this intent align to Divine Truth?

Is my protocol complete?

Do I have full permission for this intent now?

If so, say the following: "It is my intent to align my Divine Diamond Heart Crystal to this intent now."

Thank you! Thank you! Thank you!

Tone from your heart with all its glory!

And so it is!

Chapter 7: Physical Inner Children Intents

"Releasing Being Trapped"

It is my intent to create a Quantum Configuration Chamber of 955555656 to the power of 5. It is also my intent, using the Divine Colors of Liquid Orchid and Diamond Olive Green, to transmute the frequency of being trapped within my collective consciousness of physical inner children, in all dimensions, in all harmonic universes, in all galaxies and in all cubes now. I ask Lady Grace to grace any and all karma in regards to this intent. I also ask the heart of my Twin Flame, Lady Liberty, Lady Justice and the heart of my physical inner children for permission for the highest possible reality now!

Muscle test the following:

Is this intent complete?

Does this intent align to Divine Truth?

Is my protocol complete?

Do I have full permission for this intent now?

If so, say the following: "It is my intent to align my Divine Diamond Heart Crystal to this intent now."

Thank you! Thank you! Thank you!

Tone from your heart with all its glory!

And so it is!

Chapter 7: Physical Inner Children Intents

"Releasing Being a Victim"

It is my intent to create a Quantum Configuration Chamber of 977887888 to the power of 3. It is also my intent, using the Divine Colors of Liquid Daffodil and Diamond Cypress, to transmute the frequency of being a victim within my collective consciousness of physical inner children, in all dimensions, in all harmonic universes, in all galaxies and in all cubes now. I ask Lady Grace to grace any and all karma in regards to this intent. I also ask the heart of my Twin Flame, Lady Liberty, Lady Justice and the heart of my physical inner children for permission for the highest possible reality now!

Muscle test the following:

Is this intent complete?

Does this intent align to Divine Truth?

Is my protocol complete?

Do I have full permission for this intent now?

If so, say the following: "It is my intent to align my Divine Diamond Heart Crystal to this intent now."

Thank you! Thank you! Thank you!

Tone from your heart with all its glory!

And so it is!

Chapter 7: Physical Inner Children Intents

"Releasing Being a Martyr"

It is my intent to create a Quantum Configuration Chamber of 967887889 to the power of 9. It is also my intent, using the Divine Colors of Liquid Cobalt Blue and Diamond Crimson, to transmute the frequency of being a martyr within my collective consciousness of physical inner children, in all dimensions, in all harmonic universes, in all galaxies and in all cubes now. I ask Lady Grace to grace any and all karma in regards to this intent. I also ask the heart of my Twin Flame, Lady Liberty, Lady Justice and the heart of my physical inner children for permission for the highest possible reality now!

Muscle test the following:

Is this intent complete?

Does this intent align to Divine Truth?

Is my protocol complete?

Do I have full permission for this intent now?

If so, say the following: "It is my intent to align my Divine Diamond Heart Crystal to this intent now."

Thank you! Thank you! Thank you!

Tone from your heart with all its glory!

And so it is!

Chapter 7: Physical Inner Children Intents

"Releasing Being a Liar"

It is my intent to create a Quantum Configuration Chamber of 999787999 to the power of 7. It is also my intent, using the Divine Colors of Liquid Coral Pink and Diamond Electric Blue White, to transmute the frequency of being a liar within my collective consciousness of physical inner children, in all dimensions, in all harmonic universes, in all galaxies and in all cubes now. I ask Lady Grace to grace any and all karma in regards to this intent. I also ask the heart of my Twin Flame, Lady Liberty, Lady Justice and the heart of my physical inner children for permission for the highest possible reality now!

Muscle test the following:

Is this intent complete?

Does this intent align to Divine Truth?

Is my protocol complete?

Do I have full permission for this intent now?

If so, say the following: "It is my intent to align my Divine Diamond Heart Crystal to this intent now."

Thank you! Thank you! Thank you!

Tone from your heart with all its glory!

And so it is!

Chapter 7: Physical Inner Children Intents

"Releasing Being in Danger"

It is my intent to create a Quantum Configuration Chamber of 990889999 to the power of 3. It is also my intent, using the Divine Colors of Liquid Cherry and Diamond Plum White, to transmute the frequency of being in danger within my collective consciousness of physical inner children, in all dimensions, in all harmonic universes, in all galaxies and in all cubes now. I ask Lady Grace to grace any and all karma in regards to this intent. I also ask the heart of my Twin Flame, Lady Liberty, Lady Justice and the heart of my physical inner children for permission for the highest possible reality now!

Muscle test the following:

Is this intent complete?

Does this intent align to Divine Truth?

Is my protocol complete?

Do I have full permission for this intent now?

If so, say the following: "It is my intent to align my Divine Diamond Heart Crystal to this intent now."

Thank you! Thank you! Thank you!

Tone from your heart with all its glory!

And so it is!

Chapter 7: Physical Inner Children Intents

"Releasing Being Mocked"

It is my intent to create a Quantum Configuration Chamber of 933335333 to the power of 6. It is also my intent, using the Divine Colors of Liquid Chrome Yellow and Diamond White Gold, to transmute the frequency of being mocked within my collective consciousness of physical inner children, in all dimensions, in all harmonic universes, in all galaxies and in all cubes now. I ask Lady Grace to grace any and all karma in regards to this intent. I also ask the heart of my Twin Flame, Lady Liberty, Lady Justice and the heart of my physical inner children for permission for the highest possible reality now!

Muscle test the following:

Is this intent complete?

Does this intent align to Divine Truth?

Is my protocol complete?

Do I have full permission for this intent now?

If so, say the following: "It is my intent to align my Divine Diamond Heart Crystal to this intent now."

Thank you! Thank you! Thank you!

Tone from your heart with all its glory!

And so it is!

Chapter 7: Physical Inner Children Intents

"Releasing Pity"

It is my intent to create a Quantum Configuration Chamber of 994996999 to the power of 5. It is also my intent, using the Divine Colors of Liquid Yellow and Diamond Silver, to transmute the frequency of pity within my collective consciousness of physical inner children, in all dimensions, in all harmonic universes, in all galaxies and in all cubes now. I ask Lady Grace to grace any and all karma in regards to this intent. I also ask the heart of my Twin Flame, Lady Liberty, Lady Justice and the heart of my physical inner children for permission for the highest possible reality now!

Muscle test the following:

Is this intent complete?

Does this intent align to Divine Truth?

Is my protocol complete?

Do I have full permission for this intent now?

If so, say the following: "It is my intent to align my Divine Diamond Heart Crystal to this intent now."

Thank you! Thank you! Thank you!

Tone from your heart with all its glory!

And so it is!

Chapter 7: Physical Inner Children Intents

"Releasing Disapproval"

It is my intent to create a Quantum Configuration Chamber of 987899565 to the power of 3. It is also my intent, using the Divine Colors of Liquid Lemon and Diamond Peach, to transmute the frequency of disapproval within my collective consciousness of physical inner children, in all dimensions, in all harmonic universes, in all galaxies and in all cubes now. I ask Lady Grace to grace any and all karma in regards to this intent. I also ask the heart of my Twin Flame, Lady Liberty, Lady Justice and the heart of my physical inner children for permission for the highest possible reality now!

Muscle test the following:

Is this intent complete?

Does this intent align to Divine Truth?

Is my protocol complete?

Do I have full permission for this intent now?

If so, say the following: "It is my intent to align my Divine Diamond Heart Crystal to this intent now."

Thank you! Thank you! Thank you!

Tone from your heart with all its glory!

And so it is!

Chapter 7: Physical Inner Children Intents

"Releasing Forgetfulness"

It is my intent to create a Quantum Configuration Chamber of 966757999 to the power of 4. It is also my intent, using the Divine Colors of Liquid Cherry and Diamond Indigo, to transmute the frequency of forgetfulness within my collective consciousness of physical inner children, in all dimensions, in all harmonic universes, in all galaxies and in all cubes now. I ask Lady Grace to grace any and all karma in regards to this intent. I also ask the heart of my Twin Flame, Lady Liberty, Lady Justice and the heart of my physical inner children for permission for the highest possible reality now!

Muscle test the following:

Is this intent complete?

Does this intent align to Divine Truth?

Is my protocol complete?

Do I have full permission for this intent now?

If so, say the following: "It is my intent to align my Divine Diamond Heart Crystal to this intent now."

Thank you! Thank you! Thank you!

Tone from your heart with all its glory!

And so it is!

Chapter 7: Physical Inner Children Intents

"Releasing Manipulation"

It is my intent to create a Quantum Configuration Chamber of 996655757 to the power of 9. It is also my intent, using the Divine Colors of Liquid Silver and Diamond Lilac, to transmute the frequency of manipulation within my collective consciousness of physical inner children, in all dimensions, in all harmonic universes, in all galaxies and in all cubes now. I ask Lady Grace to grace any and all karma in regards to this intent. I also ask the heart of my Twin Flame, Lady Liberty, Lady Justice and the heart of my physical inner children for permission for the highest possible reality now!

Muscle test the following:

Is this intent complete?

Does this intent align to Divine Truth?

Is my protocol complete?

Do I have full permission for this intent now?

If so, say the following: "It is my intent to align my Divine Diamond Heart Crystal to this intent now."

Thank you! Thank you! Thank you!

Tone from your heart with all its glory!

And so it is!

Chapter 7: Physical Inner Children Intents

"Releasing Sorrow"

It is my intent to create a Quantum Configuration Chamber of 955777321 to the power of 3. It is also my intent, using the Divine Colors of Liquid Jade and Diamond Purple, to transmute the frequency of sorrow within my collective consciousness of physical inner children, in all dimensions, in all harmonic universes, in all galaxies and in all cubes now. I ask Lady Grace to grace any and all karma in regards to this intent. I also ask the heart of my Twin Flame, Lady Liberty, Lady Justice and the heart of my physical inner children for permission for the highest possible reality now!

Muscle test the following:

Is this intent complete?

Does this intent align to Divine Truth?

Is my protocol complete?

Do I have full permission for this intent now?

If so, say the following: "It is my intent to align my Divine Diamond Heart Crystal to this intent now."

Thank you! Thank you! Thank you!

Tone from your heart with all its glory!

And so it is!

Chapter 7: Physical Inner Children Intents

"Releasing Rape"

It is my intent to create a Quantum Configuration Chamber of 999869494 to the power of 4. It is also my intent, using the Divine Colors of Liquid Rose and Diamond Emerald Green, to transmute the frequency of rape within my collective consciousness of physical inner children, in all dimensions, in all harmonic universes, in all galaxies and in all cubes now. I ask Lady Grace to grace any and all karma in regards to this intent. I also ask the heart of my Twin Flame, Lady Liberty, Lady Justice and the heart of my physical inner children for permission for the highest possible reality now!

Muscle test the following:

Is this intent complete?

Does this intent align to Divine Truth?

Is my protocol complete?

Do I have full permission for this intent now?

If so, say the following: "It is my intent to align my Divine Diamond Heart Crystal to this intent now."

Thank you! Thank you! Thank you!

Tone from your heart with all its glory!

And so it is!

Chapter 7: Physical Inner Children Intents

"Releasing the Fear of Going Home"

It is my intent to create a Quantum Configuration Chamber of 944445646 to the power of 6. It is also my intent, using the Divine Colors of Liquid Melon and Diamond Blue, to transmute the frequency of the fear of going home within my collective consciousness of physical inner children, in all dimensions, in all harmonic universes, in all galaxies and in all cubes now. I ask Lady Grace to grace any and all karma in regards to this intent. I also ask the heart of my Twin Flame, Lady Liberty, Lady Justice and the heart of my physical inner children for permission for the highest possible reality now!

Muscle test the following:

Is this intent complete?

Does this intent align to Divine Truth?

Is my protocol complete?

Do I have full permission for this intent now?

If so, say the following: "It is my intent to align my Divine Diamond Heart Crystal to this intent now."

Thank you! Thank you! Thank you!

Tone from your heart with all its glory!

And so it is!

Chapter 7: Physical Inner Children Intents

"Releasing the Fear of Being Fat"

It is my intent to create a Quantum Configuration Chamber of 978777676 to the power of 3. It is also my intent, using the Divine Colors of Liquid Peachy Cream and Diamond Red, to transmute the frequency the fear of being fat within my collective consciousness of physical inner children, in all dimensions, in all harmonic universes, in all galaxies and in all cubes now. I ask Lady Grace to grace any and all karma in regards to this intent. I also ask the heart of my Twin Flame, Lady Liberty, Lady Justice and the heart of my physical inner children for permission for the highest possible reality now!

Muscle test the following:

Is this intent complete?

Does this intent align to Divine Truth?

Is my protocol complete?

Do I have full permission for this intent now?

If so, say the following: "It is my intent to align my Divine Diamond Heart Crystal to this intent now."

Thank you! Thank you! Thank you!

Tone from your heart with all its glory!

And so it is!

Chapter 7: Physical Inner Children Intents

"Releasing the Fear of Being Tortured"

It is my intent to create a Quantum Configuration Chamber of 998997555 to the power of 8. It is also my intent, using the Divine Colors of Liquid Lime and Diamond Aquamarine, to transmute the frequency of the fear of being tortured within my collective consciousness of physical inner children, in all dimensions, in all harmonic universes, in all galaxies and in all cubes now. I ask Lady Grace to grace any and all karma in regards to this intent. I also ask the heart of my Twin Flame, Lady Liberty, Lady Justice and the heart of my physical inner children for permission for the highest possible reality now!

Muscle test the following:

Is this intent complete?

Does this intent align to Divine Truth?

Is my protocol complete?

Do I have full permission for this intent now?

If so, say the following: "It is my intent to align my Divine Diamond Heart Crystal to this intent now."

Thank you! Thank you! Thank you!

Tone from your heart with all its glory!

And so it is!

Chapter 7: Physical Inner Children Intents

"Releasing the Fear of Speaking in Front of Large Audiences"

It is my intent to create a Quantum Configuration Chamber of 933333646 to the power of 3. It is also my intent, using the Divine Colors of Liquid Taupe and Diamond Electric Blue, to transmute the frequency of the fear of speaking in front of large audiences within my collective consciousness of physical inner children, in all dimensions, in all harmonic universes, in all galaxies and in all cubes now. I ask Lady Grace to grace any and all karma in regards to this intent. I also ask the heart of my Twin Flame, Lady Liberty, Lady Justice and the heart of my physical inner children for permission for the highest possible reality now!

Muscle test the following:

Is this intent complete?

Does this intent align to Divine Truth?

Is my protocol complete?

Do I have full permission for this intent now?

If so, say the following: "It is my intent to align my Divine Diamond Heart Crystal to this intent now."

Thank you! Thank you! Thank you!

Tone from your heart with all its glory!

And so it is!

Chapter 7: Physical Inner Children Intents

"Releasing Nightmares"

It is my intent to create a Quantum Configuration Chamber of 978777999 to the power of 9. It is also my intent, using the Divine Colors of Liquid Red and Diamond Magenta, to transmute the frequency of nightmares within my collective consciousness of physical inner children, in all dimensions, in all harmonic universes, in all galaxies and in all cubes now. I ask Lady Grace to grace any and all karma in regards to this intent. I also ask the heart of my Twin Flame, Lady Liberty, Lady Justice and the heart of my physical inner children for permission for the highest possible reality now!

Muscle test the following:

Is this intent complete?

Does this intent align to Divine Truth?

Is my protocol complete?

Do I have full permission for this intent now?

If so, say the following: "It is my intent to align my Divine Diamond Heart Crystal to this intent now."

Thank you! Thank you! Thank you!

Tone from your heart with all its glory!

And so it is!

Chapter 7: Physical Inner Children Intents

"Releasing the Fear of Being Robbed"

It is my intent to create a Quantum Configuration Chamber of 999878666 to the power of 3. It is also my intent, using the Divine Colors of Liquid Jade and Diamond Yellow, to transmute the frequency of the fear of being robbed within my collective consciousness of physical inner children, in all dimensions, in all harmonic universes, in all galaxies and in all cubes now. I ask Lady Grace to grace any and all karma in regards to this intent. I also ask the heart of my Twin Flame, Lady Liberty, Lady Justice and the heart of my physical inner children for permission for the highest possible reality now!

Muscle test the following:

Is this intent complete?

Does this intent align to Divine Truth?

Is my protocol complete?

Do I have full permission for this intent now?

If so, say the following: "It is my intent to align my Divine Diamond Heart Crystal to this intent now."

Thank you! Thank you! Thank you!

Tone from your heart with all its glory!

And so it is!

Chapter 7: Physical Inner Children Intents

"Releasing the Fear of Starving to Death"

It is my intent to create a Quantum Configuration Chamber of 999922992 to the power of 2. It is also my intent, using the Divine Colors of Liquid Orange and Diamond Green, to transmute the frequency of the fear of starving to death within my collective consciousness of physical inner children, in all dimensions, in all harmonic universes, in all galaxies and in all cubes now. I ask Lady Grace to grace any and all karma in regards to this intent. I also ask the heart of my Twin Flame, Lady Liberty, Lady Justice and the heart of my physical inner children for permission for the highest possible reality now!

Muscle test the following:

Is this intent complete?

Does this intent align to Divine Truth?

Is my protocol complete?

Do I have full permission for this intent now?

If so, say the following: "It is my intent to align my Divine Diamond Heart Crystal to this intent now."

Thank you! Thank you! Thank you!

Tone from your heart with all its glory!

And so it is!

Chapter 7: Physical Inner Children Intents

"Releasing the Fear of Spiders"

It is my intent to create a Quantum Configuration Chamber of 997988961 to the power of 6. It is also my intent, using the Divine Colors of Liquid Blue and Metallic Aquamarine, to transmute the frequency of the fear of spiders within my collective consciousness of physical inner children, in all dimensions, in all harmonic universes, in all galaxies and in all cubes now. I ask Lady Grace to grace any and all karma in regards to this intent. I also ask the heart of my Twin Flame, Lady Liberty, Lady Justice and the heart of my physical inner children for permission for the highest possible reality now!

Muscle test the following:

Is this intent complete?

Does this intent align to Divine Truth?

Is my protocol complete?

Do I have full permission for this intent now?

If so, say the following: "It is my intent to align my Divine Diamond Heart Crystal to this intent now."

Thank you! Thank you! Thank you!

Tone from your heart with all its glory!

And so it is!

Chapter 7: Physical Inner Children Intents

"Releasing the Fear of Dying"

It is my intent to create a Quantum Configuration Chamber of 999988999 to the power of 3. It is also my intent, using the Divine Colors of Liquid Pink and Diamond Autumn Wood Orange, to transmute the frequency of the fear of dying within my collective consciousness of physical inner children, in all dimensions, in all harmonic universes, in all galaxies and in all cubes now. I ask Lady Grace to grace any and all karma in regards to this intent. I also ask the heart of my Twin Flame, Lady Liberty, Lady Justice and the heart of my physical inner children for permission for the highest possible reality now!

Muscle test the following:

Is this intent complete?

Does this intent align to Divine Truth?

Is my protocol complete?

Do I have full permission for this intent now?

If so, say the following: "It is my intent to align my Divine Diamond Heart Crystal to this intent now."

Thank you! Thank you! Thank you!

Tone from your heart with all its glory!

And so it is!

Chapter 7: Physical Inner Children Intents

"Releasing the Fear of Losing Money"

It is my intent to create a Quantum Configuration Chamber of 998789233 to the power of 5. It is also my intent, using the Divine Colors of Liquid Salmon and Diamond Violet, to transmute the frequency of the fear of losing money within my collective consciousness of physical inner children, in all dimensions, in all harmonic universes, in all galaxies and in all cubes now. I ask Lady Grace to grace any and all karma in regards to this intent. I also ask the heart of my Twin Flame, Lady Liberty, Lady Justice and the heart of my physical inner children for permission for the highest possible reality now!

Muscle test the following:

Is this intent complete?

Does this intent align to Divine Truth?

Is my protocol complete?

Do I have full permission for this intent now?

If so, say the following: "It is my intent to align my Divine Diamond Heart Crystal to this intent now."

Thank you! Thank you! Thank you!

Tone from your heart with all its glory!

And so it is!

Chapter 7: Physical Inner Children Intents

"Releasing the Fear of Being Homeless"

It is my intent to create a Quantum Configuration Chamber of 997889997 to the power of 8. It is also my intent, using the Divine Colors of Liquid Wine Burgundy and Diamond Emerald Green, to transmute the frequency of the fear of being homeless within my collective consciousness of physical inner children, in all dimensions, in all harmonic universes, in all galaxies and in all cubes now. I ask Lady Grace to grace any and all karma in regards to this intent. I also ask the heart of my Twin Flame, Lady Liberty, Lady Justice and the heart of my physical inner children for permission for the highest possible reality now!

Muscle test the following:

Is this intent complete?

Does this intent align to Divine Truth?

Is my protocol complete?

Do I have full permission for this intent now?

If so, say the following: "It is my intent to align my Divine Diamond Heart Crystal to this intent now."

Thank you! Thank you! Thank you!

Tone from your heart with all its glory!

And so it is!

Chapter 7: Physical Inner Children Intents

"Releasing the Fear of Being Unloved"

It is my intent to create a Quantum Configuration Chamber of 998789944 to the power of 4. It is also my intent, using the Divine Colors of Liquid Rose and Diamond Emerald Green, to transmute the frequency of the fear of being unloved within my collective consciousness of physical inner children, in all dimensions, in all harmonic universes, in all galaxies and in all cubes now. I ask Lady Grace to grace any and all karma in regards to this intent. I also ask the heart of my Twin Flame, Lady Liberty, Lady Justice and the heart of my physical inner children for permission for the highest possible reality now!

Muscle test the following:

Is this intent complete?

Does this intent align to Divine Truth?

Is my protocol complete?

Do I have full permission for this intent now?

If so, say the following: "It is my intent to align my Divine Diamond Heart Crystal to this intent now."

Thank you! Thank you! Thank you!

Tone from your heart with all its glory!

And so it is!

Chapter 7: Physical Inner Children Intents

"Releasing Maliciousness"

It is my intent to create a Quantum Configuration Chamber of 999797484 to the power of 9. It is also my intent, using the Divine Colors of Liquid Orange and Diamond Mauve, to transmute the frequency of maliciousness within my collective consciousness of physical inner children, in all dimensions, in all harmonic universes, in all galaxies and in all cubes now. I ask Lady Grace to grace any and all karma in regards to this intent. I also ask the heart of my Twin Flame, Lady Liberty, Lady Justice and the heart of my physical inner children for permission for the highest possible reality now!

Muscle test the following:

Is this intent complete?

Does this intent align to Divine Truth?

Is my protocol complete?

Do I have full permission for this intent now?

If so, say the following: "It is my intent to align my Divine Diamond Heart Crystal to this intent now."

Thank you! Thank you! Thank you!

Tone from your heart with all its glory!

And so it is!

Chapter 7: Physical Inner Children Intents

"Releasing Being Controlled"

It is my intent to create a Quantum Configuration Chamber of 998999696 to the power of 6. It is also my intent, using the Divine Colors of Liquid Lilac and Diamond Blue, to transmute the frequency of being controlled within my collective consciousness of physical inner children, in all dimensions, in all harmonic universes, in all galaxies and in all cubes now. I ask Lady Grace to grace any and all karma in regards to this intent. I also ask the heart of my Twin Flame, Lady Liberty, Lady Justice and the heart of my physical inner children for permission for the highest possible reality now!

Muscle test the following:

Is this intent complete?

Does this intent align to Divine Truth?

Is my protocol complete?

Do I have full permission for this intent now?

If so, say the following: "It is my intent to align my Divine Diamond Heart Crystal to this intent now."

Thank you! Thank you! Thank you!

Tone from your heart with all its glory!

And so it is!

Chapter 7: Physical Inner Children Intents

"Releasing Thievery"

It is my intent to create a Quantum Configuration Chamber of 997777899 to the power of 9. It is also my intent, using the Divine Colors of Liquid Blue and Diamond White, to transmute the frequency of thievery within my collective consciousness of physical inner children, in all dimensions, in all harmonic universes, in all galaxies and in all cubes now. I ask Lady Grace to grace any and all karma in regards to this intent. I also ask the heart of my Twin Flame, Lady Liberty, Lady Justice and the heart of my physical inner children for permission for the highest possible reality now!

Muscle test the following:

Is this intent complete?

Does this intent align to Divine Truth?

Is my protocol complete?

Do I have full permission for this intent now?

If so, say the following: "It is my intent to align my Divine Diamond Heart Crystal to this intent now."

Thank you! Thank you! Thank you!

Tone from your heart with all its glory!

And so it is!

Chapter 7: Physical Inner Children Intents

"Releasing Carelessness"

It is my intent to create a Quantum Configuration Chamber of 999797999 to the power of 3. It is also my intent, using the Divine Colors of Liquid Yellow and Diamond White Gold, to transmute the frequency of carelessness within my collective consciousness of physical inner children, in all dimensions, in all harmonic universes, in all galaxies and in all cubes now. I ask Lady Grace to grace any and all karma in regards to this intent. I also ask the heart of my Twin Flame, Lady Liberty, Lady Justice and the heart of my physical inner children for permission for the highest possible reality now!

Muscle test the following:

Is this intent complete?

Does this intent align to Divine Truth?

Is my protocol complete?

Do I have full permission for this intent now?

If so, say the following: "It is my intent to align my Divine Diamond Heart Crystal to this intent now."

Thank you! Thank you! Thank you!

Tone from your heart with all its glory!

And so it is!

Chapter 8: Nurturing Your Physical Inner Child

Your little boy and/or little girl within has held traumas for a long time. Performing intents releases negative trauma energy – this is energy which needs to be replaced. Replace it by nurturing yourself.

During this time, it is important that you drink a lot of healthy water. For example, if you weigh 140 lbs, your body requires 70 ounces of water per day to meet your biological requirement. Now that you know how to muscle test, ask which water is the best for you. I personally drink Fiji water. It is important that the water you drink is fluoride-free, as the fluoride chemical compound is the same as that is found in rat poisoning.

Get yourself a couple of small rose quartz stones. You can purchase them online or at a metaphysical store. Rose quartz will align your little inner child to a frequency of being loved. Make sure you clean the stone in sea salt for three days (no water added). After the third day, take the stone out of the sea salt and blow your breath onto the stone and say out loud, "It is my intent for this stone to work for me now." This is called programming. Once your stone is programmed, don't let anyone touch it. Also, keep the stone within three feet of you 24/7. Alternate the stones. Have one cleaning as you are using the other stone. Sometimes the stone will fill up too quickly and crack, or mysteriously disappear. If it cracks, bury it.

It is important that your physical inner child feels secure during this time. A Hausmannite stone helps you dispel any attachment to the energies that have been so familiar. Because the energies of the traumas are familiar, it gives the physical inner child a false sense of security. The Hausmannite stone provides that security instead, making it easier to let go of the harmful energies of the traumas. May many blessings come to you all!

Chapter 9: Exploring the Physical Inner Childrens' Next Step

Now that you have cleared space, you are ready to rebuild your home. What is home? Home is where your heart is! Metaphorically, it is where you find your passion for life! How do you find your passion for life? Find your passion within the journey of fulfilling your Divine Purpose. "And how does one find what his/her life purpose in life is, you ask?"

Your birth date reveals your life path and New Earth Numerology reveals your Divine Purpose of your Collective Physical Inner Children. For example, if your birthday is on October 16, 1951, it can be written as 10/16/1951. Add each set of numbers as follows: The "10" is added as 1+0=**1**. The "16" is added as 1+6=**7**. The "1951" calculation is the sum of two subtotals: the first two numbers make the first subtotal: 1+9=1 (the 0 is dropped from 10), and the second two numbers make the second subtotal: 5+1=6. Now add the two subtotals: 1+6=**7**.

These three numbers create a new number: 1, 7 and 7, or **177**. In New Earth Numerology, the numbers are read backwards: 177 becomes **771**. Sevens represent spirituality. Ones represent new beginnings. Back to back numbers, such as the two sevens in our example, represent the creation of a new archetype for the world.

Therefore, in our example, the Divine Purpose is to create a new archetype for spirituality for a new beginning for the world. Now figure in a passion. In this example, Sonic Reiki can be the passion. Therefore, the final result in our example is: *Sonic Reiki is a new archetype for spirituality for a new beginning for the world.*

Knowing your life purpose keeps you focused. It becomes the road map for your journey. To receive your New Earth Numerology reading, contact Linda at *soundmaster55@verizon.net* or Tom at *master_of_light@verizon.net*.

We all are part of a Divine Plan. If we all know our Divine Purpose in life, our collective creation is heaven on earth. When this happens, we are aligned to Divine Flow. This is where our Physical Inner Children begin to trust that Divine Prosperity comes from within. In this moment, expansion of consciousness takes place. This allows space for all of our Divine Dreams to manifest into form. This is Divine Truth! How do I know this? Because I am living the Dream, and so can you!

Testimonials

Fears have hurt me in so many ways. Some ways are obvious, such as the stress and worry from having fears. Others are how I relate to others or the triggers I get because of the fears I hold. Fears affect me in ways that are not always apparent. For example, the fear of failure affects my absorption of calcium phosphate, and the fear of heights restricts what I can do.

After healing the fears in my physical inner children, I am less stressed and do not get triggered the way I used to. I now absorb calcium phosphate and I am able to look over balconies.

It is for these reasons that Linda Sylvester's book "Healing the Physical Inner Children" is a gateway to healing fears - and it is so much more. I recommend this book as a definite healing tool!

Loving Light Songsister
Richmond Hill, Ontario

I have found the book "Healing the Physical Inner Children" to be an effective and simple tool to achieve the life I desire to live. It has helped me to release the stories of my past, so that I may live more fully in the present. It has helped me to change and reframe my perception of the past, with intent to create a present life that aligns to my deepest life purpose and the freedom to love more fully. Thank you, Linda, for bringing me a tool that has helped me to choose my path to joy and to live lovingly in the present.

Louise-Anne Childerhose
Oakville, Ontario

Additional testimonial on back cover.

Bibliography

[1] Collins, Danica. "DNA Science and What Russian Researchers Have Surprisingly Discovered…." Underground Health Reporter. Under Ground Health Reporter, n.d. Web. 14 July 2012. <http://undergroundhealthreporter.com/>.

[2] Dewey, Reiko Myamoto. "More Messages in Water The Spirit of Ma'at Interviews Dr. Masaru Emoto." LifeEnthusiast - Restoring Vitality to You and to the Planet. LifeEnthusitast, n.d. Web. 14 July 2012. <http://life-enthusiast.com/usa/>.

www.ingramcontent.com/pod-product-compliance
Lightning Source LLC
Chambersburg PA
CBHW042321150426
43192CB00001B/7